T0285707

Cosmic
Self-Care

Leaping Hare Press

Cosmic Self-Care

Spiritual rituals for modern mystics

Katie Huang

Founder of ☽ LOVE BY LUNA

Illustrated by **Phe Johnson**

CONTENTS

INTRODUCTION

Self-care—it's the buzzword that's practically echoing in our ears these days, and for good reason. We all know it's important, and it sounds like something we should definitely be doing. But why is it that despite our best intentions, we often end up on the couch binge-watching TV shows or tackling our never-ending to-do lists instead of indulging in the self-care we genuinely want?

Enter your new BFF: the cosmos. Yes, you heard that right, the universe has your back, and there's undeniable magic in aligning with the universe's natural rhythms. You see, humans have always been intimately connected to the natural world. We've used the stars to navigate our journeys, observed agricultural cycles to sow and harvest, and relied on lunar cycles to anticipate the push and pull of the tides. It's in our DNA to be in sync with nature's rhythms, and not just in a metaphorical sense. Nearly all of the elements in our bodies—from the oxygen in our lungs to the calcium in our bones—were made in a star long before our planet came into existence. So, when you gaze up at the night sky, remember that you're not just observing the universe, you're a part of it, quite literally.

That said, if you feel like you're constantly chasing time to squeeze in a little self-care, don't worry. The cosmos has already marked those perfect moments for you. The movement of the stars and the changing seasons offer up plenty of pockets of opportunity for you to connect with your inner self and align with the world around you—you just have to know when to look for them. And lucky for you, this book is here to help reveal those opportune moments, making sure you never miss them again. Within these pages, you'll find a range of timelines and rituals for self-care, tailored to different cosmic rhythms and intentions. Whether you resonate with the Moon's phases, the zodiac seasons, the Wheel of the Year, planetary transits, or all of the above, this book has got you covered. Let's begin!

TIMELINES

In the realm of cosmic self-care, celestial rhythms are like our guiding stars. And you know what they say—timing is everything. So before we embark on this exciting journey, consider the following timelines for mapping out your self-care practices. Among them, you'll find various calendars that connect us with the ever-moving tapestry of the universe, from the dance of the Moon to the turning of the Wheel of the Year. What's beautiful about these sacred cycles is that they aren't just about external shifts, they're also deeply reflective of the transformations within ourselves. Picture the seasons. As nature cycles through birth, growth, decay, and rebirth, we too experience these phases in our lives. By honoring these cosmic rhythms, we tap into a deeper understanding of ourselves and our connection to the world around us. It's a reminder that we're not separate from nature, we're an integral part of it.

LUNAR CALENDAR

The Moon holds a profound space in the realm of self-care, gifting us with a natural framework for setting intentions and manifesting our desires. While each phase of the Moon carries unique energies, there are two that shine particularly bright: the new moon and the full moon.

New moons mark fresh beginnings, a cosmic clean slate where we plant the seeds of our intentions. Their energy is all about birthing ideas, setting goals, and embracing change. On the other hand, full moons radiate the culmination of our efforts, illuminating our accomplishments and shedding light on what needs releasing. They're a time of reflection, celebration, and letting go.

Here's where the Moon's capricious nature comes into play. The lunar cycle spans approximately 29.5 days, meaning the dates for each new moon and full moon shift from month to month. Subsequently, it takes about 15 days to go from the new moon to the full moon. To stay in tune with these phases, the best approach is to look up their specific dates ahead of time. It's like setting a date with the universe—a moment to synchronize your intentions with the Moon's energy.

Here's a handy tip: these lunar phases don't just pop up for one night and vanish into the ether. They graciously linger for a few days. So, feel free to perform your lunar rituals a day before, or two days after the exact date if it aligns better with your schedule or intuition. You'll still be able to harness all the magic the Moon has to offer during this period.

ZODIAC CALENDAR

The zodiac calendar follows the Sun's passage through the 12 signs, each with its unique character and energy. As the Sun moves through these signs over the course of a year, it offers us opportunities for personal growth and self-discovery by illuminating different areas of our lives and encouraging us to express various facets of our identity, from self-confidence during Leo season to introspection during Scorpio season.

Here you'll find the general dates for the zodiac seasons, but keep in mind that these can shift slightly depending on the year and your time zone. So, if you're planning your self-care rituals, it's a good idea to double-check these dates in an almanac or online. Additionally, the astrological new year begins in late March with Aries season, as Aries is the first sign of the zodiac.

Aries Season *March 21–April 19*
Aries season initiates the astrological year with a burst of dynamic energy. Ruled by the passionate and assertive Mars, it inspires confidence and action.

Taurus Season *April 20–May 20*
As Taurus season unfolds, the energy shifts to a more grounded and steady pace. Ruled by Venus, the planet of love and abundance, it highlights the pleasures of the material world.

Gemini Season *May 21–June 20*
Gemini season ushers in a sense of curiosity and versatility. Ruled by Mercury, the planet of communication, it encourages us to explore diverse interests, engage in lively conversations, and adapt to change with ease.

Cancer Season *June 21–July 22*
As Cancer season takes center stage, emotions come to the forefront. Ruled by the Moon, it deepens our connection to our inner selves and our homes.

Leo Season *July 23–August 22*
Leo season arrives with a burst of confidence and creativity. Ruled by the radiant Sun, it inspires self-expression and leadership.

Virgo Season *August 23–September 22*

Virgo season shifts the focus to practicality, organization, and attention to detail. Ruled by Mercury, it sharpens our analytical skills and encourages us to improve efficiency.

Libra Season *September 23–October 22*

Libra season ushers in a sense of balance, harmony, and beauty. Ruled by Venus, it emphasizes the importance of relationships, diplomacy, and aesthetic appreciation.

Scorpio Season *October 23–November 21*

Scorpio season brings intensity and transformation to the forefront. Co-ruled by Pluto and Mars, it delves into the depths of emotions, secrets, and regeneration.

Sagittarius Season *November 22–December 21*

As Sagittarius season unfolds, a sense of adventure and expansion takes hold. Ruled by Jupiter, the planet of abundance and growth, it encourages us to broaden our horizons, explore new territories, and seek wisdom.

Capricorn Season *December 22–January 19*

Capricorn season brings a strong focus on discipline, ambition, and practicality. Ruled by Saturn, it highlights responsibilities, long-term goals, and the pursuit of success.

Aquarius Season *January 20–February 18*

Aquarius season ushers in a spirit of innovation, individuality, and humanitarianism. Ruled by Uranus, the planet of change, it encourages us to embrace our uniqueness, advocate for social causes, and think outside the box.

Pisces Season *February 19–March 20*

Pisces season concludes the astrological year with sensitivity, compassion, and spiritual depth. Ruled by Neptune, it invites us to explore our inner realms, connect with our intuition, and dive into the world of dreams and creativity.

WHEEL OF THE
YEAR CALENDAR

The Wheel of the Year is a cycle of seasonal festivals and holidays celebrated in various Earth-based spiritual traditions. It represents the changing seasons and the natural rhythms of the Earth. The wheel typically includes eight festivals, including solstices, equinoxes, and cross-quarter days like Samhain and Beltane. Each celebration is a reflection of the Earth's journey through the year.

The Wheel of the Year begins with Samhain, as it is often considered the Celtic New Year. It's also important to note that some dates in the Wheel of the Year, such as Ostara and Yule, may vary slightly each year depending on astronomical calculations. The equinoxes and solstices are influenced by celestial events, and as a result, their dates may shift by a day or two from year to year. It's essential to check astronomical calendars for the exact dates of these celebrations for a particular year.

SAMHAIN *October 31–November 1*
Samhain marks the end of the harvest season and the beginning of winter. It's a time when the veil between the physical and spiritual world is thin, making it ideal for honoring ancestors and practicing divination. To celebrate, people may carve pumpkins, light candles in jack-o'-lanterns, and dress in costumes to ward off malevolent spirits.

YULE *December 20–23*
Yule, or the winter solstice, celebrates the return of the Sun's light as days begin to lengthen. It's a time for embracing hope, rebirth, and the triumph of light over darkness. People often decorate their homes with evergreen wreaths, light candles, and exchange gifts. The Yule log, a symbol of the returning Sun, is burned in a hearth or fireplace.

IMBOLC *February 1–2*
Imbolc falls midway between the winter solstice and the spring equinox. It signifies the awakening of life and the stirrings of nature beneath the cold earth. It's a time for purification rituals, house blessings, and making plans for the coming spring.

OSTARA *March 20–23*

Ostara, the spring equinox, is a moment of balance when day and night are equal. It signifies the arrival of longer, sunnier days and the blossoming of life. Traditionally, people may plant seeds or engage in activities that celebrate fertility and renewal. It's a time to cleanse your living space, set intentions for growth, and reconnect with the Earth's awakening energies.

BELTANE *April 30–May 1*

Beltane welcomes the full arrival of spring and is often seen as a celebration of fertility, love, and passion. It's a time to honor the union of the god and goddess, symbolized by the maypole dance and the lighting of bonfires. Couples may jump over fires for purification and to strengthen their bond.

LITHA *June 20–23*

Litha, or the summer solstice, marks the zenith of the Sun's power. It's the longest day and shortest night of the year. Litha is a time for celebrating abundance, honoring the Earth's beauty, and expressing gratitude for the season's blessings. It's a perfect moment for outdoor rituals, divination, and harnessing the Sun's transformative power.

LUGHNASADH *August 1*

Lughnasadh, or Lammas, heralds the beginning of the harvest season. People celebrate by making corn dollies, baking bread, and sharing the first fruits of the harvest. Lughnasadh's energy encourages reflection on personal achievements and setting intentions for the rest of the season.

MABON *September 20–23*

Mabon, the fall equinox, marks the second moment of balance in the Wheel of the Year. As the days grow shorter, it's a time for introspection, gratitude, and seeking balance in your own life. Mabon encourages acknowledging both light and darkness within yourself.

PLANETARY CALENDAR

In astrology, each planet is said to govern a different area of life and personality. When aligning self-care rituals with the planets, there are a couple of key timing opportunities to consider.

Firstly, you can choose to perform rituals when the planets change zodiac signs. This is significant because as a planet moves from one sign to another, it brings a shift in energy and focus. For example, when Venus moves from analytical Virgo to harmonious Libra, it's a great time to focus on relationships and balance. Each planetary sign change represents a shift in the areas of life that the planet's energy influences.

Secondly, you can align your rituals with planetary retrogrades. During retrograde periods, a planet's energy turns inward, often prompting reflection, reevaluation, and revisiting of matters related to that planet's influence. For instance, when Mercury goes retrograde, it's an ideal time for introspection and refining communication skills.

Thirdly, you can co-ordinate your rituals with different days of the week, known as planetary days, to enhance their potency. Each day of the week is associated with a particular planet, drawing on the energy and attributes of that celestial body. Timing your rituals with planetary days can create a sense of synchronicity with the cosmos and amplify their effectiveness. Note: Uranus, Neptune, and Pluto do not have designated days in traditional astrology because they were discovered after the development of these systems. The equinoxes and solstices, which determine the seasonal shifts, are influenced by celestial events, and as a result, their dates may shift by a day or two from year to year. It's essential to check astronomical calendars for the exact dates of these celebrations for a particular year.

Please note that the time spent in retrograde can vary slightly depending on the specific retrograde cycle. The above information provides a general overview of the planets' movements and retrograde periods, but it's best to research current transits to pinpoint exact dates. By observing these planetary transitions, you can tap into the unique qualities and energies associated with each planet's movements.

PLANET	Meaning & Governance	Frequency of Sign Change	Time Spent in Retrograde	Planetary Day
SUN	Core essence, ego, individuality, self-expression, vitality, life purpose	Approximately 30 days	Does not retrograde	Sunday
MOON	Emotions, instincts, subconscious mind, emotional responses, intuition, nurturing	Approximately 2.5 days in each zodiac sign	Does not retrograde	Monday
MERCURY	Communication, intellect, mental processes, thinking, learning, writing	Approximately 14–30 days	About 3–4 times a year, for about 3 weeks each time	Wednesday
VENUS	Love, beauty, harmony, relationships, art, aesthetics, values	Approximately every 23–24 days	About once every 1.5 years, for about 6 weeks	Friday
MARS	Action, energy, assertiveness, drive, passion, courage	Approximately every 1.5–2 months	About once every 2 years, for about 2 months	Tuesday
JUPITER	Expansion, abundance, growth, knowledge, wisdom, spirituality	Approximately every 12–13 months	About once a year, for about 4 months	Thursday
SATURN	Discipline, responsibility, limitations, structure, commitment, personal growth	Approximately every 2.5 years	About once a year, for about 4.5–5 months	Saturday
URANUS	Change, innovation, rebellion, individuality, sudden insights	Approximately every 7 years	About once a year, for about 5–6 months	None
NEPTUNE	Dreams, intuition, spirituality, creativity, illusion, subconscious mind	Approximately every 14 years	About once a year, for about 5–6 months	None
PLUTO	Transformation, power, deep psychological processes, regeneration	Approximately every 12–31 years	About once a year, for about 5–6 months	None

SAMHAIN

YULE

MABON

IMBOLC

LAMMAS

OSTARA

LITHA

BELTANE

WHEEL OF
THE YEAR RITUALS

If you're new to self-care rituals, I highly recommend starting with the Wheel of the Year. While lunar phases and zodiac seasons certainly offer their own unique magic, the Wheel of the Year provides a broader perspective and a gentler pace, which can be especially welcoming for beginners.

One of the key advantages is the timing. With lunar phases, you have rituals every month, sometimes even twice a month with the new moon and full moon. Similarly, the zodiac seasons shift roughly every month. In contrast, the events in the Wheel of the Year occur approximately every one-and-a-half months, allowing for a bit more spaciousness in your self-care practice.

Moreover, the Wheel of the Year celebrates the interconnectedness of our lives with the environment, encouraging us to honor the Earth's rhythms. Whether it's planting seeds in spring, harvesting in fall, or reflecting in the depths of winter, these rituals remind us that we are part of something much larger and more magnificent than ourselves.

SAMHAIN

Altar Ritual for Ancestral Wisdom

October 31–November 1

Of all the ancient festivals, few are as steeped in history, mystery, and magic as Samhain. A precursor to modern Halloween, Samhain is traditionally observed from sunset on October 31 to sunset on November 1. This point in the year marks the end of the harvest season and the beginning of winter. During Samhain, it is believed that the veil between the living and the spirit world grows thin, allowing a special connection with the other side.

At its core, Samhain is a celebration of death and the wisdom it offers. While this may sound eerie or unsettling, it's an acknowledgment of the inevitability of change and transformation. Death, in this context, is not an end but a transition—a passage of one state of being to another. Just as the trees release their leaves and the world takes on a temporary cloak of decay during Samhain, we too must let go of what no longer serves us.

Materials:

- A small table or surface
- Photographs or mementos of loved ones who have passed
- A white candle
- A glass of water
- Offering of food or drink (something your loved ones enjoyed)
- Matches or a lighter
- Pen and paper

Directions:

Place the photos or mementos at the center of the table or surface. Surround it with the white candle, a glass of water, and your offering of food or drink. Light the white candle, saying a few words to invite your ancestors to join you. Visualize their presence and open your mind to their guidance.

Sit quietly in front of the altar, close your eyes, and take a few deep breaths. Imagine your loved ones surrounding you, offering their support and wisdom. Offer the food or drink to your ancestors while speaking their names aloud and expressing your love and gratitude. Write down any messages or insights that come to you during this time. Close the ritual by thanking your ancestors for their presence, then snuff out the candle. Leave the offerings out for a day or two as a sign of respect, or refresh them as desired.

YULE

Return of the
Light Ritual for Hope
December 20–23

Yule, often celebrated around December 21, marks the winter solstice—the longest night of the year. It's a time when the Sun begins its triumphant return, promising longer days and the renewal of life. Yule reminds us that even in the coldest and darkest times, there's a glimmer of light and warmth waiting to be reborn.

Yule is a time for gatherings with loved ones, sharing tales, and feasting on the bounties of the season. Many traditions involve lighting a Yule log, often a large piece of oak, which is slowly burned throughout the night. Additionally, evergreen plants such as holly, ivy, and mistletoe are used for decoration—symbolizing the continuity of life in the midst of winter's chill. Wreaths made from these plants can be hung as protective talismans.

Materials:

- A small candle
- A fireproof dish or holder
- Matches or a lighter
- Pen and paper

Directions:

Find a quiet space within your home, dimly lit. Come to a seated position and take a few deep breaths. Place the candle in the center of your space on a fireproof dish or holder. As you light it, say, "With this flame, I ignite the light within and without." Take a moment to draw or write a symbol representing the Sun on a small piece of paper. Place the paper near the candle, symbolizing the Sun's return and your connection to the season. Turn off all other lights and sit in the soft glow of your candle. Meditate on the warmth and hope it represents, allowing its light to fill you with renewed energy.

Reflect on your aspirations for the coming year, focusing on the personal growth and the light you wish to bring to your life and the world. Close the ritual by saying, "As the Sun is reborn, may my inner light shine brightly. Blessed Yule!" If possible, allow the candle to burn down on its own, or snuff it out before you go to bed. Never leave a lit candle unattended.

IMBOLC

Seeds of Inspiration
Ritual for Growth

February 1–2

Imbolc is an ancient Celtic holiday that marks the awakening of the earth from its winter slumber and the first signs of spring. It is typically observed from sundown on February 1 and continues through February 2. During Imbolc, chilly temperatures, snowy grounds, and barren branches can make the surrounding landscape look dull and lifeless. However, things are not what they seem. Just as seeds are germinating in the darkness, new ideas and inspirations are quietly stirring within us, taking form. This is a time when the creative potential we've nurtured in the quiet of winter starts to manifest, like the first sprouts breaking through the frozen soil. Ultimately, Imbolc reminds us that even in the harshest of seasons, there is a hidden vitality and promise of renewal not only in nature, but also in our own lives. It encourages us to have patience and faith in the emergence of these new beginnings and the growth of our creative endeavors.

Materials:

- A candle
- Matches or a lighter
- A small pot or container
- Potting soil
- Seeds (representing your creative ideas or inspirations)

Directions:

Begin by lighting the candle. As the flame flickers, take a moment to center and ground yourself. Hold the pot or container in your hands, feelings its energy and connection to the earth. Fill the pot with potting soil, symbolizing the fertile ground in which your ideas will take root. As you do this, say, "In the darkness of winter, I plant the seeds of my inspiration, knowing that they will flourish in due time." Then carefully plant the seeds in the soil, one by one, with intention and care. As you do this, envision your creative ideas taking form and growing into something beautiful and meaningful.

Place the pot near the lit candle, allowing its warmth to represent the fire of your creativity and passion. Safely extinguish the candle when you are ready to close out the ritual. Keep the pot in a warm, well-lit place and continue to tend to it regularly as your ideas grow and take shape.

OSTARA

Altar for
New Beginnings
March 20–23

As winter loosens its icy grip, we welcome the return of the warmth and light with Ostara—the spring equinox. This celebration typically falls around March 20 or 21, and signifies the official arrival of spring in the Northern Hemisphere. After months of rest and introspection, this shift invites us to re-engage with the physical world and start planting the seeds of our intentions, both literally and metaphorically. As we witness nature's rebirth with buds and blossoms, Ostara invites us to align ourselves with the flourishing earth and embrace the magic of new beginnings. Day and night are also nearly equal at this time, emphasizing themes of balance and renewal.

Materials:

- A bowl of potting soil
- A half empty eggshell
- A tealight candle
- A piece of green aventurine
- A piece of citrine
- A piece of rose quartz
- Wildflowers petals
- Matches or a lighter

Directions:

Find a peaceful outdoor spot or sunny window sill to connect with nature's energy. Begin setting up your materials by placing the bowl of potting soil in front of you and nestle the half empty eggshell within it. Carefully place the tealight candle inside the eggshell (you may need to use a large egg in order for it to fit). Surround the eggshell with green aventurine for growth, citrine for joy, and rose quartz for harmony. Sprinkle wildflower petals of your choosing around the crystals, visualizing your intentions taking root and blossoming with vibrant energy.

Light the tealight candle as you speak your intention for new beginnings aloud, such as, "With the return of spring, I release the old and heavy. I embrace the fresh and new." Watch the candle flicker and crystals glisten, feeling their renewing energies fill you with new life. Allow the candle to burn out on its own or snuff it out when desired.

BELTANE

Fire Flower Ritual for Transformation

April 30–May 1

Beltane is a sacred festival held on May 1, marking the peak of spring and the coming of summer. Its name comes from the Gaelic word meaning "bright fire". Beltane is often called the "Maypole" festival, where a tall pole is erected and adorned with ribbons. Dancers, representing the god and goddess, weave intricate patterns around the Maypole, symbolizing the sacred union between masculine and feminine energies. This union represents the creative force behind all life, both in nature and within ourselves. It's a celebration of love, desire, and the power of creation. While Beltane and Ostara both share themes of fertility and growth, Beltane differs in that it leans into the more passionate and amorous aspects of life. That said, Beltane is a powerful time to ignite your passions, get your creative juices flowing, and reclaim or reconnect with your own sexual energy.

Materials:

- A bundle of fresh or dried flowers
- Pen and paper
- Red, orange, or pink ribbon
- Matches or a lighter
- A fireproof dish or holder

Directions:

Begin by venturing outdoors to a quiet and serene spot, preferably under the open sky. Alternatively, if conducting the ritual indoors, choose a well-ventilated area. Hold the bundle of fresh or dried flowers in your hands as you meditate on the aspects of your life you wish to transform or release. Reflect on these thoughts and emotions.

Take a piece of paper and write down the things you'd like to transform or release, using clear and concise language. Tie the paper securely to the bundle of flowers using a red, orange, or pink ribbon, representing the fiery energies of Beltane.

Carefully ignite the flower bundle with a match or lighter, then place it in the fireproof dish or holder. Allow the bundle to burn completely. As it turns to ashes, envision your intentions dissolving into the universe, ready for renewal. Close the ritual with a deep breath, feeling lighter and freer. Dispose of the ashes by returning them to the earth or scattering them in the breeze.

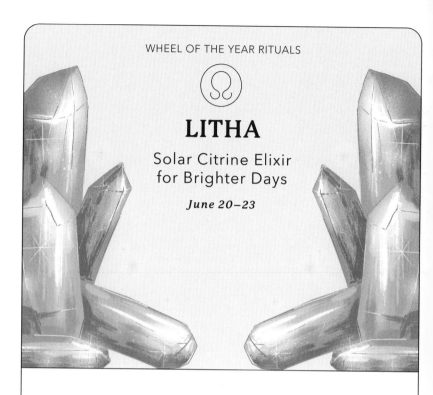

LITHA

Solar Citrine Elixir
for Brighter Days

June 20–23

Litha, also known as Midsummer or the summer solstice, marks the longest day and shortest night of the year in the Northern Hemisphere. Celebrated around June 21, it's a time when the Sun, at its zenith, represents the peak of life's energy and abundance. If spring is when we awaken, then summer is the season when we are fully alive. It's a time for joy, celebration, and gratitude for the blessings we've received. Just as the seeds we planted and nurtured in the previous months are now in full bloom, this festival embodies the realization of our intentions and the acknowledgment of the good we have in our lives. Ultimately, Litha is a celebration of light, both internal and external, inviting us to reflect on our own inner radiance.

Materials:

- A clear glass container with a lid
- Clean drinking water
- A piece of citrine

Directions:

Find a tranquil outdoor setting where you feel the Sun's energy. Place the clear glass container there. Fill the container with clean drinking water, symbolizing the element of water and its nurturing qualities. Hold the citrine crystal in your hand and connect with its joyful energy. Close your eyes and take a few deep breaths to center yourself.

Visualize the Sun's rays infusing the citrine with its life-giving power and strength, filling it with a golden light. Place the crystal into the container, allowing its energy to infuse the water with positive vibrations. Hold the container in your hands and set your intention for the solar-charged water by saying, "Abundance is my birthright. I was born to receive it." Seal the container with its lid and leave it in direct sunlight for a few hours, allowing the Sun and citrine to fully charge the water.

Afterward, remove the crystal from the container and take a few small sips of the solar-charged water. Visualize the water filling you with abundance and nourishing your body. Drink the remaining water throughout the day to revitalize your spirit, or use it in spells or rituals to strengthen your intentions.

LUGHNASADH

Bread Blessing Ritual for Spiritual Nourishment

August 1

Lughnasadh, also known as Lammas, is celebrated around August 1, signifying the first harvest of the year, typically of grains such as wheat and barley. This is an important time in nature, as we begin to see the fruits of our labor manifest in the physical realm. All of the effort we've put into this growing season (which began back at the winter solstice) is beginning to pay off, and that's something worth celebrating, so use this moment to pause and take pride in your hard work. You might feel like you haven't done much up to this point, but that's entirely untrue! While there is still more work to finish, don't dismiss or downplay the progress you've made. Additionally, the heat of the summer Sun will help to "ripen" your remaining harvests, bringing a flow of vital energy that will support you in achieving your goals.

Materials:

- Pen and paper
- A small loaf of bread (homemade or store-bought)
- A plate
- A bottle of olive oil
- A pinch of salt

Directions:

Gather your materials in front of you in a quiet space. Close your eyes and reflect on what you're harvesting this year in your life. Consider the progress you've made and growth you've experienced over the past few months. What challenges have you overcome? What are you proud of? Write down your thoughts on a piece of paper and set it aside.

Take the loaf of bread in your hands and say, "I bless this bread as a symbol of the harvest." Break off a piece of the blessed bread and place it on the plate. Drizzle a few drops of olive oil over the bread, symbolizing the richness of the earth, and say, "I honor the abundance in my life." Sprinkle a pinch of salt over the bread for purification and protection and say, "I cleanse my body and spirit."

Eat the blessed bread slowly, focusing on its nourishment and allowing it to fill you with a sense of gratitude. Carry the piece of paper with your reflections on you as a reminder of your progress.

MABON

Energy Spray Ritual for Decluttering Your Life

September 20–23

Mabon, or the fall equinox, is typically celebrated around September 21 or 22, marking the second harvest of the year. Historically, this was a time to give thanks for the fruits of the harvest and to prepare for the colder months ahead. Signifying a turning point of the seasons, Mabon emphasizes the balance and transition from equal daylight and nighttime to longer nights. As the first day of the "dark half of the year" (fall and winter), Mabon is the perfect opportunity to get introspective and take stock of what we've reaped the past months, whether they be physical, emotional, or spiritual dividends. While it's important to hold gratitude for the positives, it's essential for us to recognize and release the things that are no longer serving our growth.

Materials:

- Mint tea (prepared and cooled)
- A sprayer bottle
- A sprig of fresh mint
- Tea tree essential oil
- A small piece of clear quartz

Directions:

Begin in a quiet, clutter-free space. Brew a cup of mint tea and let it cool to room temperature. Take a few deep breaths to center yourself. Acknowledge the clutter, both physical and energetic, that you wish to release. This can include limiting beliefs, old attachments, or bad habits. Pour the cooled mint tea into the sprayer bottle. Add the sprig of fresh mint, symbolizing purification and growth. Then, add a couple of drops of tea tree essential oil for cleansing.

Hold the clear quartz crystal in your hand and infuse it with your intention to clear negativity and obstacles that hinder your growth. Visualize it radiating pure, cleansing energy. Place the clear quartz crystal into the sprayer bottle with the other ingredients, saying, "Clear quartz, amplify this spray's cleansing power." Close the sprayer bottle and shake it gently to charge it. Hold the bottle and visualize the clutter, negativity, and obstacles dissolving as you spray the mixture throughout your space. Store the bottle in the refrigerator after use for up to a week, or until the mint begins to show signs of decay.

ZODIAC RITUALS

Just like the Wheel of the Year, the zodiac seasons represent a cycle, but with a different perspective. While the Wheel of the Year focuses on nature's annual journey— birth, growth, harvest, and rest—the zodiac seasons delve into the subtler aspects of life.

With the zodiac, we're navigating the ever-revolving celestial sphere. Each season mirrors the cycle of birth, growth, maturity, and transformation in our inner world. Aries marks the beginning, igniting the fire of new intentions. Taurus settles in, anchoring us to earthly pleasures. As we progress, we embody the spirit of each sign, moving one step further in our journey of self-discovery and personal evolution. In this section, we'll explore how to harness these zodiac energies for self-care, turning each season into an opportunity for growth and healing.

BOLD AND FEARLESS

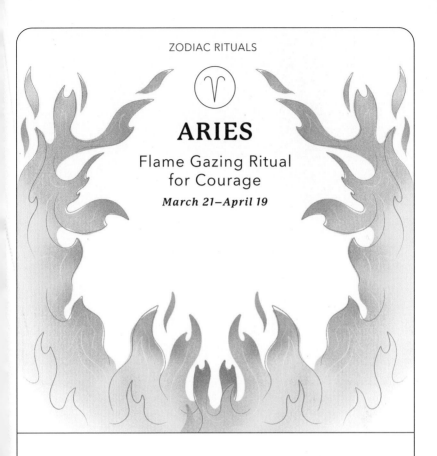

ARIES

Flame Gazing Ritual for Courage

March 21–April 19

Aries season bursts forth with dynamic energy, igniting our inner flames of courage and determination. This is a time of bold beginnings, giving us the spark of inspiration for our goals. As the fiery spirit of Aries takes hold, it's the perfect backdrop for a flame gazing ritual, harnessing the season's fearless energy to embolden our hearts and propel us toward our ambitions with unwavering confidence.

Materials:

- A red candle
- A piece of bloodstone
- Matches or a lighter

Directions:

Begin the ritual in a quiet, dimly lit space. Place the red candle and bloodstone crystal in front of you. Take several deep breaths to center yourself, then light the red candle, saying,

"I KINDLE THIS FLAME TO INVOKE THE FIERY COURAGE OF ARIES WITHIN ME."

Gaze into the flame, allowing its warmth and light to fill you with confidence and courage.

Hold the crystal and connect with its sturdy, grounding energy. Then say,

"BLOODSTONE, GRANT ME STRENGTH AND RESILIENCE."

Repeat the affirmation,

> ## "I AM BOLD AND FEARLESS. I EMBRACE CHALLENGES WITH CONFIDENCE. MY COURAGE KNOWS NO BOUNDS."

Close your eyes and reflect on the areas of your life where you need courage. Journal your thoughts, intentions, and the actions you'll take. Thank the flame and crystal for their energies. Snuff out the candle, knowing that your courage is now kindled.

TAURUS

Spell Jar Ritual
for Money

April 20–May 20

While Aries season gave us powers of initiation, Taurus season allows our ideas to take root in the physical world. A patient earth sign, Taurus embodies stable, grounded, and practical energy. During this time, there's a focus on building security, both financially and emotionally. It's an ideal period for working diligently toward long-term goals, establishing routines, and enjoying life's sensual pleasures. A money spell jar ritual harmonizes perfectly with this energy, amplifying intentions for wealth and abundance as we embrace the steadfast determination of the bull.

Materials:

- Incense (optional)
- A small glass jar with lid
- An orange peel
- A dried bay leaf
- A sprig of mint (fresh or dried)
- A small piece of green aventurine
- A small piece of pyrite

Directions:

Purify your tools by smoke cleansing them with incense or visualizing a purifying white light enveloping them. This step clears any negative energy and prepares them for your intention. Layer the bottom of the jar with orange peel for prosperity, bay leaf for abundance, mint for financial growth, green aventurine for luck, and pyrite for success. As you add each element, visualize your financial goals manifesting.

Seal the jar with the lid and hold it in your hands. Take a moment to focus your energy and state your intention aloud, such as, "Money flows freely and effortlessly to me. My life is rich and full." Gently shake the jar to activate its energy, then place it in a visible spot in your home, ideally near sources of money (such as a wallet or safe) or your workspace. Revisit the jar every few days and give it a shake to reaffirm your intent. Remember to express gratitude for the abundance that is flowing into your life as you work toward your financial goals.

MY

VOICE

IS

POWERFUL

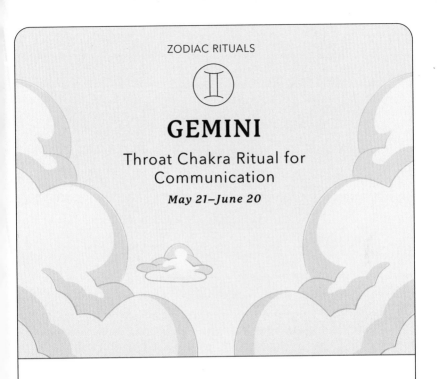

GEMINI

Throat Chakra Ritual for Communication

May 21–June 20

The transition from Taurus to Gemini season ushers in a shift from earthly indulgence to mental stimulation and social connection. This period brings a sharper, more expansive energy, encouraging outward exploration. Communication is also a central element of this season, making it ideal for learning, networking, and connecting with diverse perspectives.

Working with the throat chakra can be especially beneficial during this time, as balancing it allows us to articulate our thoughts and emotions clearly, fostering better connections and self-expression. If you struggle with connecting to your inner voice, use this ritual to dissolve communication blocks and let yourself be heard.

Materials:

- A blue crystal (such as aquamarine, blue lace agate, or lapis lazuli)
- Pen and paper

Directions:

Find a peaceful place in your home where you won't be disturbed. Sit comfortably with your back straight and hold your crystal in your hands. Close your eyes and take several deep breaths. Visualize a vibrant blue light surrounding your throat area, expanding with each breath to clear any blockages or tension. Repeat positive affirmations related to self-expression and communication, such as,

"I SPEAK MY TRUTH WITH EASE. MY VOICE IS POWERFUL. MY WORDS ARE IMPORTANT."

Take the crystal and hold it over your throat as you use your voice to heal. Hum or chant the "OM" (or "AUM") sound, feeling its vibrations resonate in your throat to release stagnant energy ("OM" is considered a sacred sound in Hindu, Buddhist, and other spiritual traditions and is believed to be a universal, primordial sound from which all other sounds and creation emerge). After a minute or two, take a moment to write down any thoughts, emotions, or ideas that may have gotten dislodged in the process. Allow your words to flow freely, without judgment or expectation. Close the ritual by thanking the universe for the healing and clarity you've received. Keep the crystal close to you and meditate with it whenever you feel at a loss for words.

CANCER

Home Spray Ritual for Security

June 21–July 22

As Gemini season's mentally charged energy fades, Cancer season moves us toward the depths of our emotions, infusing our lives with a nurturing and sensitive energy. During this time, our focus turns inward, emphasizing the importance of family, home, and emotional connections. Much like the protective crab that retreats into its shell, we too crave comfort and security at this time. That said, crafting a protection spray is a great way to promote a sense of safety in our sacred spaces during this tender and heartfelt season.

Materials:

- A small spray bottle
- Filtered or purified water
- Sea salt or pink Himalayan salt
- A few drops of essential oil (such as sage, rosemary, or cedar wood)
- A small piece of clear quartz

Directions:

Fill the spray bottle with filtered or purified water, leaving a bit of space at the top. Add a pinch of sea salt or Himalayan salt to purify the energy. Then, add a few drops of your chosen essential oil for protection. Hold the clear quartz crystal in your hand and focus on your intention to protect your home. Visualize a bright, protective light surrounding your space, sealing all the windows and doors.

Place the crystal into the spray bottle. Close your eyes and take a few deep breaths. Concentrate on the energy of your home and visualize it as a safe and secure place. Hold the spray bottle and say, "With this elixir, I seal my home in protection and love. May only positive energies reside within these walls." Walk through each room of your home, spraying a fine mist in the air. Focus on entryways, windows, and corners, imagining a protective barrier forming. Return to your starting point and express gratitude for the protection you've invoked. Store the spray bottle in a cool, dark place for up to 6 months, using it whenever you feel the need to cleanse and safeguard your space again.

FILLED WITH THE POWER OF THE SUN

LEO

Sun Salutation Ritual for Positive Vibes

July 23–August 22

After the cozy embrace of Cancer season, Leo season invites us to leave our comfort zone and encourages us to step into the spotlight. The need to be seen, heard, and appreciated takes center stage now. It's a time to showcase our talents, embrace self-confidence, and seek recognition. Leo season also encourages us to pursue our passions, take bold risks, and express our unique talents, making it an ideal time for creative endeavors, self-discovery, and basking in the joy of life's grandeur.

In this ritual, you'll learn how to harness the strength of the Sun—Leo's ruling planet—by moving through a few Sun Salutation yoga poses. Please note that this is an abbreviated version. Sun Salutations typically consist of longer sequences with more poses, and you can find these online if you wish to expand your practice.

Materials:

- A quiet, sunlit space
- Comfortable clothing
- A yoga mat or soft surface

Directions:

Choose a sunny morning to perform this ritual. Start by standing tall on your mat, facing the Sun if possible. Take a moment to center yourself, then begin to flow through a mini series of Sun Salutation yoga poses to synchronize your movements with the Sun's energy.

Start with Mountain Pose (Tadasana). Stand tall with feet hip-width apart and arms at your sides. Engage your thighs, lengthen your spine, and roll your shoulders back and down, finding balance and stability in the pose. Inhale deeply as you raise your arms overhead, palms together. Feel your body stretch and reach for the sky, drawing in the Sun's strength.

Move into Upward Salute (Urdhva Hastasana). Exhale as your gently arch your back and lean back slightly, basking in the Sun's glow. Imagine absorbing its warmth and vitality.

Transition to Standing Forward Bend (Uttanasana). Inhale, then exhale as you fold forward at your hips, reaching for the ground. Feel your body release tension, like the Sun's rays melting away stress.

As you move through these poses, incorporate a simple affirmation that resonates with you. For example, you can repeat,

"I AM FILLED WITH THE POWER OF THE SUN."

At the end of your practice, stand still, facing the Sun with your eyes closed. Gently lift your gaze toward the Sun, feeling its warmth and brightness infusing you with renewed energy and positivity.

EFFORT YIELDS
GREAT REWARDS

VIRGO

Simmer Pot Ritual for Productivity

August 23–September 22

As we make the shift from Leo season's vibrant main stage, we step into the meticulous post-production of Virgo season. This season encourages us to refine and analyze our creations, to turn our passion into a precise craft. It's a time of practicality, organization, and attention to detail. This energy can be harnessed for self-improvement, health, and fine-tuning the projects we initiated last month.

During this time, we're invited to address the finer aspects of life, set realistic goals, and perfect our work. That said, an easy way to fill your home and spirit with positive, productive energy this season is by using a simmer pot. Not only will it create an atmosphere of concentration and alignment, but it makes your home smell delicious!

Materials:

- A pen and a notebook
- A small saucepan or pot
- Water
- Fresh rosemary and basil (for focus)
- Citrus slices (for clarity)
- Cinnamon sticks (for motivation)
- A bay leaf (for achievement)

Directions:

Begin by clarifying your intentions for productivity during Virgo season. Write down your goals in the notebook. Fill the saucepan or pot with water and bring it to a boil on the stove. Once boiled, set the temperature to low heat and add your ingredients to the pot. Stir clockwise to combine. As the pot simmers, mediate on your intentions. Gaze at the rising steam, envisioning yourself successfully completing tasks and projects with ease. Repeat a Virgo-themed affirmation aloud, such as,

"I AM INDUSTRIOUS, ORGANIZED,
AND DISCIPLINED.
MY CONSISTENT EFFORTS
YIELD GREAT REWARDS."

Allow the pot to simmer until its aroma fills your entire home. This can take as little as 10 minutes, or be done over 2—3 hours if desired (adding additional water if necessary). When you're done, turn off the heat and let everything cool. Strain the mixture into a spray bottle and spritz it around your home to promote mental focus when needed.

LIBRA

Venus Altar Ritual
for Harmony

September 23–October 22

While Virgo season taught us to focus on detail-oriented tasks, practicality, and self-improvement, Libra season shows us the importance of balance, harmony, and co-operation. Virgo's precision is now complemented by Libra's grace, as we shift from individual self-improvement to the refinement of our social interactions.

This season is ideal for improving relationships, both personal and professional, and for considering the perspectives of others. It's an opportunity to seek beauty, create art, and appreciate the aesthetics in life. Libra's energy prompts us to bring more equilibrium into our lives and make choices that enhance the harmony of our inner and outer worlds. In this ritual, you'll set up an altar dedicated to Venus—Libra's ruling planet—to promote love, beauty, and relationships.

Materials:

- A pink or green altar cloth
- A small table or surface
- A small mirror or a picture of Venus
- Rose quartz crystals or rose petals
- Matches or a lighter
- Red or pink candles
- Incense (jasmine or rose) and a holder
- Your favorite perfume or essential oil
- A small dish of honey or rosewater
- Fresh flowers or potted plants

Directions:

Place the altar cloth on your chosen surface. Position the picture or mirror in the center. Arrange rose quartz crystals or rose petals around it. Light the candles and incense, sparking your connection to Venus. Apply your chosen perfume or essential oil, (focusing on your pulse points), awakening your sensual side. Place the dish of honey or rosewater on the altar as an offering to Venus, symbolizing your desire for sweetness in love and relationships. Decorate the altar with fresh flowers or potted plants, celebrating Venus's connection to nature and beauty.

Sit in front of the altar and meditate on your desires related to love and beauty. Speak your intentions aloud, inviting Venus's energy into your life. Close the ritual by thanking Venus for her presence and guidance. Allow the candles and incense to burn out on their own, or snuff them out if you must. Keep the altar as a loving and harmonious focal point in your space. Regularly refresh the offerings and maintain it with care.

SCORPIO

Tarot Spread Ritual for Shadow Work

October 23–November 21

As we move from the balance-seeking nature of Libra season, we enter the transformative and intense energies of Scorpio season. This season encourages us to embrace our passions, shed old patterns, and seek the truth in all aspects of life. The current energy is intense and emotional, offering opportunities for healing and rebirth. It's a time to confront our fears, let go of what no longer serves us, and emerge stronger and wiser.

Shadow work can be particularly useful during this time, as Scorpio's piercing intuition helps us in unearthing and integrating feelings we've suppressed or ignored. Use this illuminating tarot spread ritual to shine a light on your hidden aspects and unconscious fears as you delve into the depths of your psyche.

Materials:

- A piece of malachite
- Your preferred tarot deck
- A pen and a journal

Directions:

Find a tranquil space and come to a seated position. Hold the malachite crystal and focus on your intention for the shadow work—to uncover and heal hidden aspects of yourself. Shuffle your tarot deck while reflecting on the areas of life you wish to explore. When ready, draw three cards for the spread.

Turn over the first card, which represents "The Shadow Aspect." Examine this card to uncover the hidden aspects or unresolved issues. Ask yourself: "What have I been avoiding or denying?"

Turn over the second card, which represents "The Healing Message." Reflect on this card to understand the guidance or message it offers for healing and integration. Ask yourself: "What steps can I take to address and heal my shadow aspect?"

Turn over the third card, which represents "The Transformation." This card represents the potential for transformation and growth that comes from facing your shadow. Ask yourself: "How can I embrace and integrate these aspects to become a more whole and authentic version of myself?"

As you work through the spread, allow yourself to feel and release any buried emotions or patterns. Write down your thoughts and insights, carrying your newfound understanding and healing with you.

SAGITTARIUS

Travel Sachet Ritual
for Protection

November 22–December 21

While Scorpio season taught us how to navigate the depths of our shadows, Sagittarius season represents a return to the light. Sagittarius season carries an adventurous, optimistic, and expansive energy. It's a time for broadening our horizons, embracing freedom, and seeking higher knowledge. This season encourages us to explore, learn, and share our wisdom with others, making it an excellent period for travel and self-discovery.

As you journey far and wide, carrying a travel protection sachet on you is a must. In this ritual, you'll learn how to create one with a few simple ingredients to safeguard your adventures and ensure safe and spirited travels.

Materials:

- A small, clean cloth or sachet bag
- Dried rosemary or basil
- A small piece of black tourmaline
- A coin
- A personal item that represents you (such as a piece of jewelry or a photo)

Directions:

Find a quiet, undisturbed space and focus your energy on an upcoming journey (or your daily commute) and the desire for protection while traveling. Begin to add your ingredients to the cloth or sachet bag, one by one. Use dried rosemary or basil for protection, black tourmaline for grounding, a coin for good luck, and a personal item to connect you to the spell. As you place the items in the bag, visualize a protective bubble of white light surrounding you, growing larger and brighter with each item. Close the sachet tight and hold it in your hands as you say, "I am safe and protected at all times. Wherever I go, only good things happen."

Keep the sachet with you throughout your travels, whether in your vehicle, bag, or pocket. It will serve as a protective talisman, allowing you to explore the world with peace of mind.

DOORS ARE
OPENING
FOR ME

CAPRICORN

Spell Jar Ritual for Career Success

December 22–January 19

If Sagittarius season inspired us to dream big, then Capricorn season helps us make our dreams a reality with its disciplined and determined energy. Capricorn season, falling in the heart of winter, is an ideal time for focused ambition and practical goal-setting. It encourages us to take a structured approach to our aspirations and long-term plans. During this season, we are inspired to tackle our responsibilities and ambitions with determination and persistence. It's an opportune period to build a strong foundation for future success, whether in our careers or personal lives. Capricorn energy supports organization, financial planning, and career advancement. In this ritual, you'll learn how to boost your career aspirations and manifest success with this empowering spell jar, designed to propel your professional growth.

Materials:

- A small glass jar with a lid
- A piece of carnelian
- A piece of lapis lazuli
- A piece of pyrite
- Dried lavender buds
- White or brown sugar
- A green or blue ribbon

Directions:

Start in a quiet, clutter-free space. Focus your thoughts on your career goals, envisioning success and fulfillment. Begin layering the jar with the crystals, lavender buds, and sugar, visualizing your intentions as you add each one. Close the jar tightly and hold it in your hands. Visualize a radiant green or blue light surrounding it, infusing it with your career aspirations and desires. Secure the jar with a green or blue ribbon, symbolizing abundance and wisdom. Gently shake the jar as you speak an affirmation for your career aloud, such as,

"I AM WORTHY OF SUCCESS. DOORS ARE OPENING FOR ME."

Place the jar on your work desk or a spot where you'll see it daily. Whenever you need a boost, hold the jar, and visualize your career goals with unwavering confidence. Keep the jar on display as a powerful reminder of your intentions. Refresh the herbs and crystals periodically to maintain their energy.

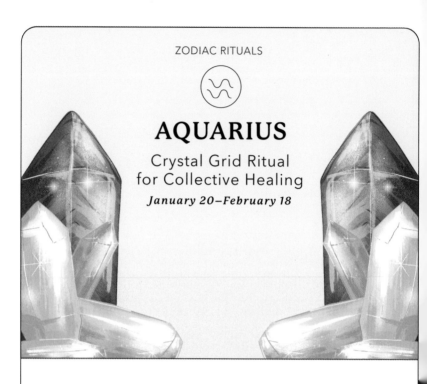

AQUARIUS

Crystal Grid Ritual for Collective Healing

January 20–February 18

As we transition from the structured, goal-oriented realm of Capricorn season, we step into the unconventional and visionary energy of Aquarius season. Capricorn is known for its disciplined and pragmatic approach, emphasizing hard work and traditional values, while Aquarius season brings a breath of fresh air. It's a shift from the conventional to the avant-garde, from earthly practicality to intellectual exploration. In Aquarius season, we're encouraged to embrace innovation, think outside the box, and question the status quo. The emphasis is on individuality, community, and a greater concern for humanitarian issues. Crafting a crystal grid for collective healing is a wonderful way to honor Aquarian energy at this time, as it promotes peace, co-operation, and unity among all beings.

Materials:

- A small table or surface
- Pen and paper
- A large piece of selenite
- 3 pieces of amethyst
- 3 pieces of rose quartz
- 3 pieces of clear quartz

Directions:

Find a small table or surface to create the crystal grid. Write an intention expressing your desire for peace, harmony, and healing within the general collective (or specific communities that you're a part of) on a piece of paper. Place this statement at the center of your chosen surface, then place the large selenite crystal on top of it. This will serve as the anchor point for your crystal grid. Arrange the pieces of amethyst, rose quartz, and clear quartz in a circle around your intention (alternating the stones) to promote a sense of unity and co-operation.

Close your eyes and visualize a radiant, soothing energy emanating from the crystal grid, enveloping the world in peace and compassion. After a minute, turn your focus to your written intention, feeling its energy rippling through all beings and the planet itself. Open your eyes and activate the grid by tracing it with your finger three times, imagining that energy is shooting out through the tip like a beam of light. Leave the grid in place for as long as you like, allowing it to continuously radiate healing energy to the collective.

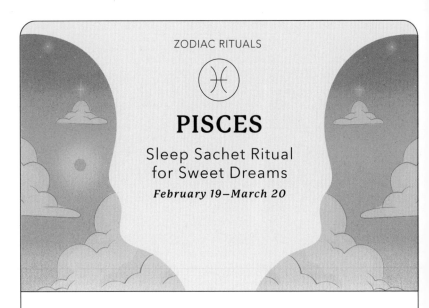

PISCES

Sleep Sachet Ritual
for Sweet Dreams

February 19–March 20

Leaving behind the innovative and community-focused energy of Aquarius season, we embark on a journey into the dreamy and empathetic realm of Pisces season. While Aquarius season encourages us to think outside the box, Pisces season ushers in an atmosphere of ethereal intuition and deep emotional exploration. This transition invites us to shift from the analytical and logical to the intuitive and compassionate. It's a time to explore our inner landscapes, connect with our feelings, and dive into the mystical realms of spirituality and artistic expression. Pisces season encourages us to embrace our dreams, creativity, and the deeper mysteries of life, offering a sense of unity with the cosmos and the emotional depths of our souls.

Making a sleep sachet during this season is a wonderful ritual, as it harmonizes with Pisces' introspective spirit, enhancing deep sleep, vivid dreams, and spiritual connection during these ethereal and introspective nights.

Materials:

- Pen and paper
- A small cloth sachet bag
- 1 tbsp dried lavender
- 1 tbsp dried chamomile
- 1 tbsp dried rosemary
- A small piece of amethyst
- A small piece of lepidolite
- 1/2 tsp sea salt

Directions:

Choose a serene space and dim the lights. Sit comfortably. Set your intention for a night of deep, restorative sleep and pleasant dreams. Write this intention on the piece of paper and place it in the sachet bag. Add in the dried lavender for relaxation, chamomile for reducing insomnia, and rosemary for warding off nightmares. Hold the amethyst and lepidolite crystals in your hand and visualize calming and emotionally balancing energy flowing into them. Add them to the bag and sprinkle the sea salt on top for additional purification and protection.

Tie the sachet bag securely. Hold it close and take a deep breath, feeling a sense of tranquility. Recite your intention aloud as you visualize your sleep becoming deeper and more rejuvenating. Place the sachet under your pillow or near your bedside for a night of undisturbed rest.

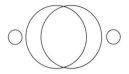

LUNAR RITUALS

Change truly is the only constant in life, isn't it? And there's no cosmic force that reflects this lesson better than the Moon. Much like our nightly companion, we too are in constant motion, shifting through various phases. That said, lunar rituals resonate beautifully with our own evolution. They offer a powerful opportunity to connect with the fluidity of our emotions, intentions, and desires. Whether we're setting fresh intentions during a new moon or releasing what no longer serves us under a full moon, these rituals mirror the ebb and flow of our own transformations, and rhythmic journey of our lives.

In this section, you'll find nourishing rituals for each new moon (as it travels through the zodiac signs), monthly Farmer's Almanac full moons, and even special celestial events such as blue moons, black moons, and eclipses. As you perform them, remember to trust the process, knowing that every phase holds unique gifts. Be patient with yourself, and above all, let your intuition be your guide.

NEW MOON IN ARIES

Affirmation Ritual
for Personal Empowerment

The new moon in Aries symbolizes fresh starts, courage, and assertive energy. As the first sign of the zodiac, Aries encourages us to take action and embrace a can-do attitude. During this new moon, we may feel more confident and ready to tackle obstacles than usual, making it a potent time for setting intentions, making plans, and taking the first steps toward our goals. That said, crafting a personal affirmation during this lunation can empower you to harness Aries' bold spirit, kickstarting new ventures, and embracing challenges with determination.

Materials:

- Matches or a lighter
- A candle
- Pen and paper
- Crystals or objects symbolizing your intention
- A fireproof dish or holder

Directions:

Find a serene space where you won't be disturbed. Light a candle to signify the illumination of your new path. Close your eyes, take a few deep breaths, and reflect on the new beginning you desire. What positive changes do you seek? Write your intention on the paper. With your intention in mind, create a powerful, present-tense affirmation that embodies your goals. Make it concise, positive, and personal, such as, "I am the architect of my destiny." Hold the crystals or objects in your hands, infusing them with your intention and the energy of your affirmation. Speak your affirmation aloud, repeating it at least three times with conviction. Visualize your new beginning unfolding. Burn the paper with your intention over the candle flame (safely) and drop into a fireproof dish or holder as a symbol of releasing it to the universe. Let go of any doubts or fears.

Express your gratitude for the fresh start and newfound empowerment. Carry the charged crystals or objects with you as a reminder of your affirmation. Repeat this ritual as needed to reaffirm your commitment to your new beginning.

SUPPORTED BY THE EARTH

NEW MOON IN TAURUS

Root Chakra Ritual for Grounding

The new moon in Taurus carries a powerful and stabilizing energy, providing an ideal moment to connect with the Earth's nurturing force. This lunar phase is all about grounding, prosperity, and stability. Under Taurus' influence, we're encouraged to take a step back, evaluate our resources, and secure our foundations. By conducting a root chakra ritual during this lunation, you can firmly anchor your intentions into the fertile soil of your life. This act of grounding allows you to connect with your innate power, fostering a sense of unwavering stability in your pursuits.

Materials:

- A red or black candle
- Patchouli or cedarwood essential oil
- A red or black crystal (such as red jasper or black tourmaline)
- A comfortable chair or cushion

Directions:

Find a quiet, uncluttered space where you won't be disturbed. Sit comfortably on your chair or cushion. Close your eyes, take several deep breaths, and visualize yourself connecting with the Earth's core. Feel its stable, grounding energy rising up through your feet. Anoint the red or black candle with a few drops of patchouli or cedarwood essential oil for strength and protection. Use a small brush or cotton swab to rub the oil onto the candle in a clockwise motion. Light the candle, symbolizing the root chakra's element of fire. Repeat a grounding affirmation, such as,

"I AM SAFE, ROOTED, AND SUPPORTED BY THE EARTH'S ENERGY."

Hold the red or black crystal in your hand, infusing it with your intention for grounding and stability. Close your eyes and focus on your breath. Visualize a red, swirling energy at the base of your spine, expanding and grounding you. Chant the root chakra's mantra,

"LAM"

(pronounced "lum" as in plum) allowing its vibrations to resonate within you. Express gratitude for the Earth's support and the stability you've invoked, then extinguish the candle.

NEW MOON IN GEMINI

Idea Jar Ritual for Inspired Exploration

The new moon in Gemini embodies curiosity, communication, and exploration. This is an excellent time for pursuing new hobbies, expanding your knowledge, and connecting with others in meaningful ways. Crafting an idea jar is a wonderful way to make use of this inquisitive energy, allowing you to explore diverse subjects, ideas, and perspectives in a playful manner.

Materials:

- A piece of citrine
- A piece of green aventurine
- A piece of moonstone
- A pen and scraps of paper
- A glass jar with a lid

Directions:

Begin by holding each crystal one by one, envisioning their energy infusing your intentions. Citrine sparks enthusiasm, green aventurine fosters growth, and moonstone signifies fresh beginnings. On the scraps of paper, jot down subjects, topics, or project ideas that intrigue you, even if they seem unrelated or unconventional. Trust your instincts. Place the crystals at the bottom of the jar. Fold the pieces of paper and as you add each to the jar, visualize the subjects or ideas coming to life and leading you on exciting journeys of exploration.

Seal the jar and gently shake it to activate its energy. Set the jar in front of you and pull out one piece of paper. This becomes your focus for the new moon. Dedicate time to dive deeply into the chosen subject. Read, research, create, or brainstorm ideas related to it. Allow your curiosity to lead the way. At the day's end, record your discoveries and insights. How did this exploration inspire you? What new ideas emerged? Continue this ritual daily or as often as you like. Over time, watch your creativity and inspiration flourish.

NEW MOON IN CANCER

Moon Water Ritual for Emotional Healing

The new moon in Cancer invites us to turn our focus inward, emphasizing emotional nurturing and self-care. It encourages us to explore our feelings, set intentions related to home and family life, and deepen our emotional well-being. Crafting moon water during this time offers a meaningful way to honor this energy, fostering emotional healing and self-care through the soothing lunar influence.

Materials:

- A clean glass jar with a lid
- A white or silver cloth
- A piece of clear quartz
- Filtered or purified water

Directions:

On the evening of the new moon, choose a serene outdoor location if possible, or a window sill with direct moonlight. Place the jar on the white or silver cloth. Rinse the clear quartz crystal under water to remove any debris, then hold it between your palms. Visualize it absorbing the Moon's gentle energy. Place the cleansed crystal into the jar. Fill the jar with filtered or purified water, covering the crystal completely. Hold the jar between your hands and set an intention for your moon water, focusing on emotional healing, self-care, or any specific emotional needs.

Seal the jar and place the moonstone crystal on top of the lid to enhance its connection to the Moon. Leave the jar under the moonlight overnight. In the morning, it should be energetically charged and ready for use. You can use your moon water in a couple of ways: add a few drops to your bath, sprinkle it around your home, or simply drink it to imbue yourself with the soothing, nurturing energy of the Moon. When stored in a clean, airtight container in a cool, dark place, your moon water should last several months to a year.

EMBRACING

MY INNER

BEAUTY

NEW MOON IN LEO

Hydrating Hair Mask Ritual for Radiance

The new moon in Leo embodies confidence, creativity, and bold enthusiasm. This lunar phase encourages you to shine, take center stage, and express your authentic self. It's an ideal time to focus on boosting self-esteem and showcasing your unique talents. Crafting a hydrating hair mask provides both a bit of pampering and an opportunity to nurture your inner radiance and self-worth. Additionally, Leo is symbolized by the lion, which is often depicted with a majestic and flowing mane, so use this ritual to tame your tresses and indulge in some luxurious yet budget-friendly self-care.

Materials:

- A bowl and spoon
- 1 ripe avocado
- 2 tbsp coconut oil
- 1 tbsp honey
- A shower cap

Directions:

Mash a ripe avocado in a bowl and mix it with 2 tablespoons of coconut oil and 1 tablespoon of honey. Blend until smooth. Lightly dampen your hair with warm water, ensuring it's not soaking wet. As you apply the mask, focus on your intentions for self-worth and confidence. Say aloud or silently,

"I AM WORTHY OF LOVE AND RESPECT. I EMBRACE MY INNER BEAUTY AND RADIATE CONFIDENCE."

Massage the mask into your hair, starting at the roots and working down to the tips, imbuing it with your positive affirmations. Put on a shower cap to trap heat and enhance absorption.

Leave the mask on for at least 20 minutes, allowing the nourishing ingredients and your intentions to penetrate. During this time, meditate, read, or practice self-care to enhance relaxation. After the wait, rinse your hair thoroughly, then shampoo and condition as usual. As you rinse, express gratitude for the nourishment and self-worth you've cultivated.

NEW MOON IN VIRGO

Broom Ritual for Energetic Cleansing

The new moon in Virgo offers an ideal opportunity for cleansing and alignment. It's a wonderful time for refining your plans, setting goals, and creating order in your life. This energy can be harnessed for activities like decluttering your space, fine-tuning your routines, and grounding your intentions into practical actions.

A great way to accomplish this is with a broom ritual—a practice that not only purifies your space but also melts away stress. As you sweep away physical and emotional clutter, you'll create a harmonious environment that feels organized, refreshed, and in sync with Virgo's meticulous and grounded energy.

Materials:

- Matches or a lighter
- A white candle
- Salt
- A broom
- Incense

Directions:

Begin in a clean, clutter-free space. Light a white candle to symbolize purity and positive energy. Stand in the center of the room. Take a few deep breaths, grounding yourself. Sprinkle a thin line of salt across the doorway to create a protective barrier. Starting at the farthest corner of the room, use the broom to sweep gently toward the doorway. Visualize the negative energy being swept away and dissolving. As you sweep, chant or repeat an affirmation such as, "With this broom, I sweep away all negativity, making room for positivity and light." Sweep the negative energy out the door, crossing the salt line.

With the room cleansed, extinguish the candle, expressing gratitude for the process. Take a moment to observe the newfound lightness and relaxation in the space. Dispose of the salt, ensuring it's removed from your living area, and cleanse your broom. If you wish to invite fresh energy in, open windows, or utilize incense to smoke cleanse the area, sealing the space with positive energy and welcoming a sense of renewal.

EQUILIBRIUM
IS MY PRIORITY

NEW MOON IN LIBRA

Balance Tarot Spread for Inner Harmony

The new moon in Libra heralds an opportunity for balance and harmony. Its energy urges us to seek equilibrium in all aspects of our lives, from our relationships to our inner thoughts. One wonderful way to tap into this harmonious energy is through a tarot spread. In this ritual, you'll use the following tarot spread to support introspection and help you identify areas where you might need to strike a balance or make a compromise. If you struggle with people pleasing or setting firm boundaries, this ritual will help you reassess your priorities with ease.

Materials:

- Your preferred tarot deck
- A piece of black tourmaline
- A piece of clear quartz

Directions:

Take a few deep breaths to clear your mind and find your center. Shuffle the tarot deck, keeping in mind the question,

"WHAT AREAS OF MY LIFE NEED BALANCE?"

Repeat the question in your mind as you continue to shuffle the deck, allowing it to guide your intentions. After a minute or so, draw two cards from the deck. The first card symbolizes what needs to be released from your life, and the second represents what you should welcome more of.

Focus on the meaning of the first card as you hold the black tourmaline crystal in your hands. Connect with its detoxifying energy, and contemplate how to actively shed what is no longer beneficial in your life. Be honest with yourself. Transition to the clear quartz, embracing the meaning of the second card. Connect with its amplifying properties and explore ways to integrate this positive element into your life.

Conclude the ritual by crafting an affirmation centered around balance. For instance, you might declare,

"EQUILIBRIUM IS MY PRIORITY."

To further integrate the energies of the crystals into your life, position the black tourmaline on the right side of your bed (as you lie in bed), and clear quartz on the left side.

MY
INTUITION
IS A
GUIDING
LIGHT

NEW MOON IN SCORPIO

Sea Goddess Altar for Harnessing Intuition

The new moon in Scorpio carries deep, transformative energy that influences us to delve into our hidden emotions, confront our fears, and undergo profound personal changes. It's an ideal time for inner healing, releasing emotional baggage, and rebirthing ourselves.

To embrace Scorpio's watery depths, consider creating a sea goddess altar. As you assemble it, focus on connecting with your emotions, exploring your inner ocean, and inviting emotional healing and intuition into your life. This altar serves as a symbolic gateway to Scorpio's powerful waters, facilitating self-discovery and transformation in alignment with the new moon's energies.

Materials:

- A small bowl of water
- A plate
- A pinch of salt
- 1 tbsp dried jasmine buds
- Seashells, sand, or other items that represent the water element
- Blue crystals (such as aquamarine or blue calcite)

Directions:

Set up your altar in a serene and quiet space. Place the small bowl of water on the plate as the central focus. Add the salt to the water for purification and dried jasmine for divine insights. Surround the bowl with seashells, sand, or other decorations connected to the water element to enhance the sea's presence. Integrate blue crystals on the altar to boost intuition and clear communication, such as aquamarine, lapis lazuli, or blue calcite.

Once your altar is prepared, sit before it, close your eyes, and envision yourself peacefully floating on the ocean's surface, fully attuned to the powerful energies that surround you. As you meditate, repeat the affirmation,

"MY INTUITION IS A GUIDING LIGHT. I TRUST IN ITS POWER."

Allow silence to permeate the room as you remain in a receptive state, open to intuitive messages and insights that may come your way. Visit this altar regularly to strengthen your intuition and tap into the profound depths of Scorpio's energy, gaining a better understanding of your inner self and the mysteries of life.

FOLLOWING MY BLISS

NEW MOON IN SAGITTARIUS

Vision Board
Ritual for Bringing
Adventures to Life

The new moon in Sagittarius ushers in an energy of expansion, optimism, and adventure. It inspires us to embrace new experiences, seek wisdom, and broaden our horizons. This lunar phase is the perfect time for setting intentions related to travel, education, personal growth, and exploring the unknown.

Creating a vision board during the new moon in Sagittarius can be a powerful way to manifest your dreams and aspirations. By visually representing your goals and desires, you align your consciousness with the lunar energy, making your adventurous dreams more tangible. Whether it's images of far-off destinations, inspirational quotes, or symbols of personal growth, your vision board acts as a constant reminder of your intentions, fueling your journey toward exciting and expansive experiences. Embrace this energy and let your dreams take flight.

Materials:

- Matches or a lighter
- A yellow or orange candle
- Magazines
- Scissors
- Corkboard or poster
- A piece of green aventurine
- A piece of citrine
- A piece of carnelian
- A glue stick or tape

Directions:

Gather your materials in a clean, quiet space. Light a yellow or orange candle for Sagittarian energy. Gaze into the flame as you reflect on your bucket list—the places you want to visit and the adventures you desire. Flip through magazines and select images that resonate with your travel aspirations. Cut them out. Begin arranging the images on your corkboard or poster, adding destination names, quotes, or personal affirmations.

Meditate with your crystals in hand for a minute, then place them on your vision board to infuse it with their unique energies. Arrange them in a way that feels harmonious to you.

As you place each stone, envision your adventures coming to life in detail. Recite an affirmation such as,

"I AM CREATING
THE LIFE I DESIRE.
I AM FREE TO
FOLLOW MY BLISS."

Glue or tape everything in place, sealing your intentions. Extinguish the candle. Hang your vision board in a prominent place to continuously inspire you to seek new experiences.

WORKING TOWARD MY GOAL

NEW MOON IN CAPRICORN

Visualization Ritual for Professional Growth

The new moon in Capricorn is associated with diligent and disciplined energy. It influences our lives by encouraging us to set practical goals, work hard, and lay the foundation for long-term success. This lunar phase is an excellent time for setting career-related intentions, financial planning, and developing a structured approach to your ambitions.

A visualization ritual during the new moon in Capricorn can be a powerful tool for achieving professional growth. Visualization allows you to see yourself achieving milestones, excelling in your field, and feeling the sense of accomplishment, which in turn helps you take practical steps toward your desired success during this lunar phase.

Materials:

- Pen and paper
- A piece of garnet

Directions:

Find a peaceful space, free from distractions. Sit or lay down and close your eyes. Take a few deep breaths to center yourself. Begin to focus on your long-term career goals. Envision where you'd like to be professionally in ten years' time. Visualize your future accomplishments, your honed skills, and the positive impact you've made. Dive deep into the details, making these mental images as vivid and clear as possible. Allow the emotions associated with your success to flow through you. Imagine the feelings of fulfillment, achievement, and pride.

After a few minutes of visualization, gently open your eyes and take a moment to jot down your thoughts, feelings, and any insights that arose during your contemplation. Reflect on whether you were completely honest with yourself about what you desire and whether you could dream even bigger. Explore the reasons behind these feelings.

Now, turn your focus to your career goals and the steps required to make them a reality. Place the piece of garnet on your written vision as a symbol of your commitment. Recite an affirmation such as,

"I AM DEDICATED TO MY LONG-TERM SUCCESS, AND I PERSISTENTLY WORK TOWARD MY GOALS."

Keep the garnet with you as a tangible reminder of your intentions and a source of motivation on your path to achieving your dreams.

NEW MOON IN AQUARIUS

Smoke Cleansing Ritual for Authenticity

The new moon in Aquarius carries an energy of innovation, independence, and forward thinking. It inspires us to break free from the constraints of convention and embrace our unique visions. Our differences are what make us beautiful, and this new moon wants us to own who we truly are. Setting intentions related to personal growth, community involvement, and progressive change is encouraged at this time.

One way to honor this energy is through a smoke cleansing ritual, which aligns seamlessly with the air element associated with Aquarius. Smoke cleansing, typically done with sage or other herbs, involves burning the dried plant material and using the smoke to cleanse and purify a space. This ritual is believed to clear stagnant or negative energies, allowing fresh, positive vibes to take their place.

Materials:

- Dried herbs or flowers of your choice
- A blue ribbon
- A fireproof dish or holder
- Matches or a lighter

Directions:

Choose a quiet outdoor space or well-ventilated indoor area to perform the ritual. Gather dried herbs or flowers that intuitively call to you. Garden sage, lavender, and rosemary are excellent options for truth and cleansing, but use whatever resonates with you personally. Gently bundle the chosen herbs and flowers together to create a smoke cleansing wand, securing them with a blue ribbon. Set an intention to release limiting beliefs and embody authenticity such as, "I let go of false narratives and embrace my true self." As you speak your intention aloud, carefully light one end of the smoke cleansing wand. Allow it to burn for 30 seconds then blow it out.

Waft the fragrant smoke around your body three times, focusing on areas of tension or insecurity. Visualize the smoke purifying your aura and carrying negative energy away. Place the wand on a fireproof dish or holder to continue burning and express gratitude for this cleansing experience.

NEW MOON
IN PISCES

Enchanting Bath Ritual
for Dreaming Big

The new moon in Pisces brings an energy of heightened intuition, dreaminess, and emotional sensitivity. During this time, our moods may be deeply influenced by our subconscious, and we may find ourselves more compassionate and empathetic. It offers an ideal opportunity to set intentions related to spiritual growth, creative endeavors, and connecting with your inner self.

Embracing the element of water is crucial during this lunar phase, given Pisces' association with this element. Water symbolizes the deep currents of emotion, intuition, and the flow of life. Taking a bath ritual during this period can be a soothing and immersive way to connect with Pisces' energies. Adding herbs, essential oils, or crystals to your bath can enhance the experience, allowing you to tune in to your inner world, release emotional baggage, and receive greater spiritual insights.

Materials:

- 1 cup Epsom salts
- Lavender essential oil
- A piece of amethyst

Directions:

Create a tranquil ambiance in your bathroom by dimming the lights, allowing a sense of calm to permeate the space. As you fill your bath, dissolve a cup of Epsom salts into the warm water, enhancing your relaxation with its mineral-rich properties. Add a few drops of lavender essential oil to further soothe your mind and spirit.

Hold the amethyst crystal in your hands and take a few deep breaths, letting its peaceful energy flow through you. Imagine stress and worry dissolving as you connect with the crystal's soothing vibrations. Slowly immerse yourself in the bath, placing the amethyst nearby so it can enhance the water's energy.

As you soak, focus your thoughts on your boldest dreams and visualize them manifesting in your life. Repeatedly affirm, "I dream big, and the universe wholeheartedly supports my grandest visions." Allow these positive intentions to wash over you as you enjoy your bath, surrounded by the energy of your dreams. After your bath, drain the tub and let yourself drip dry, as this allows the magical effects of your dream-related intentions to seep into your skin. Place the amethyst crystal on your nightstand or beneath your pillow to promote peaceful dreams.

RELEASE
THE OLD,
EMBRACE
THE NEW

FULL WOLF MOON

Transformation Ritual for Personal Growth

The full Wolf Moon, occurring in January, derives its name from Indigenous American folklore, signifying the howling of hungry wolves in the winter night. This moon carries a potent, primal energy, serving as an opportune period to shed old habits and usher in intentions for the upcoming year. Like the tenacious wolf, it encourages self-reflection and emboldens you to confront life's trials with courage. This ritual guides you in letting go of outdated patterns, embracing your ever-evolving self, and nurturing personal growth and renewal as you align with the resilient spirit of the wolf.

Materials:

- Matches or a lighter
- A white candle
- Pen and paper
- A piece of clear quartz
- Fireproof dish or holder

Directions:

Find a quiet, serene space and light the white candle, symbolizing purity and illumination. Take a series of deep breaths, centering your energy and focusing your intention with each one. Write down the aspects of yourself or your life that you wish to transform or release on a piece of paper. Be honest and specific.

Hold the clear quartz crystal in your hand, allowing its energy to amplify your intent. Recite a powerful affirmation such as,

"I RELEASE THE OLD, I EMBRACE THE NEW,"

feeling its resonance course through you. With the candle's flame, safely ignite the piece of paper, vividly visualizing the old patterns and limitations turning to ash.

Carefully transfer the paper to a fireproof dish or holder to continue burning. In the ensuing stillness, meditate on the transformation happening within you, sensing the weight of the past lifting like a veil. Hold the clear quartz in your hand and visualize your intentions for your renewed self taking root. Feel the crystal amplifying your inner strength. Express gratitude for the changes occurring and the path of growth you've embarked upon. Close out the ritual by safely extinguishing the candle.

I HONOR
MY NEEDS

FULL SNOW MOON

Fire Cider Ritual for Winter Wellness

The full Snow Moon, gracing our skies in February, takes its name from the snowy landscapes of winter. It radiates calming and introspective energy, inviting us to reflect, recharge, and find solace in the stillness of the season. This moon is an ideal time for self-care, inner exploration, and setting intentions for emotional balance and renewal as we await the coming spring. In this ritual, you'll create a batch of immune-boosting fire cider—a potent non-alcoholic tonic to keep you warm and strong during the cold months.

Materials:

- 1 medium onion, chopped
- 10 garlic cloves, crushed or chopped
- 1 cup (240 g) fresh ginger root, grated or chopped
- 1 lemon, sliced
- 1 orange, sliced
- 2–3 jalapeño peppers, sliced or 1/2 tsp cayenne powder
- 3 cinnamon sticks
- 3 sprigs of fresh rosemary
- 6 sprigs of fresh thyme
- 1 cup (240 g) fresh horseradish root, chopped
- 1 tbsp dried turmeric
- 2 qt (2 litre) mason jar with a lid
- Parchment or wax paper (optional)
- 3–4 cups (720–960 ml) unfiltered apple cider vinegar
- A fine mesh strainer or cheesecloth
- 1/4 cup (60 ml) raw honey or agave syrup (or more, if desired)

Directions:

Gather the ingredients in a clean space. As you begin, focus on your intention for robust health throughout the winter season. As you grate and chop the fruits, vegetables, and herbs, imbue each with your heartfelt wishes.

Repeat this affirmation to yourself throughout this process,

"I LOVINGLY CARE FOR MY BODY AND HONOR ITS NEEDS."

Combine all of the prepared ingredients (except for the honey) in a glass mason jar. Fill the jar to the brim with apple cider vinegar so that all the ingredients are completely covered. Seal the jar tightly with a plastic lid, repeating your affirmation. If using a metal lid, place a piece of parchment or wax paper between the jar and lid before sealing to prevent the vinegar from corroding the metal. Store the jar in a cool, dark place for 4–6 weeks, shaking it daily.

After 4–6 weeks, strain the liquid into a clean jar using a fine mesh strainer or cheesecloth, adding honey to taste. Consume a tablespoon of your fire cider daily and say,

"I NOURISH AND STRENGTHEN MYSELF,"

to boost your immune system and invigorate your spirit throughout winter. For optimal freshness, store your fire cider in an airtight jar in the refrigerator, where it can be preserved for up to 6 months.

FULL WORM MOON

Spring Cleaning Ritual for Renewal

The full Worm Moon, appearing in March, heralds the emergence of earthworms as a sign of spring's arrival. This moon exudes vibrant, growth-oriented energy, inspiring us to shed the old and embrace renewal. It's a perfect time for setting intentions related to personal growth, starting new projects, and aligning with the seasonal shift toward rejuvenation. A spring-cleaning ritual can help you cleanse your space and spirit of stagnant energy and invite fresh opportunities into your life.

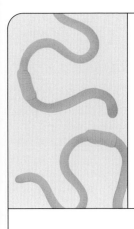

Materials:

- Matches or a lighter
- A white or green candle
- 1/2 cup (120 ml) purified water
- 1/2 cup (120 ml) white vinegar
- A spray bottle
- Your favorite essential oil
- Additional cleaning supplies

Directions:

Gather your supplies and create a calm atmosphere in your space. Light a green or white candle, its gentle flicker representing the spark of new beginnings. As the candle's flame dances, take a moment to establish your intention for the ritual, envisioning the stagnant energy dispersing and making way for vibrant, fresh energies to enter your life.

To facilitate the cleansing process, prepare a natural cleaning solution in a spray bottle by blending equal parts water and white vinegar. Add a few drops of your preferred essential oil—perhaps lavender for purification, or invigorating lemon for a refreshing ambiance. As you commence cleaning, do so with intention and awareness, seeing the dust and debris as metaphors for old energies. Imagine these negative influences being methodically swept away. Tackle clutter, donate unused items, and make space for new opportunities. Open windows to invite fresh air and energy into your space. As you complete your cleaning, extinguish the candle, saying, "I welcome purity and freshness into my space. May the energies of renewal and growth fill every corner, bringing positivity into my life."

FULL PINK MOON

Spell Jar Ritual for Self-Love

The full Pink Moon, gracing our skies in April, emanates a vibrant and nurturing energy. Named for the pink springtime flowers that dot the landscape, it symbolizes growth, renewal, and the emergence of life from the depths of winter. This lunar phase inspires us to embrace themes of love, compassion, and personal development. It's a period for tending to the gardens of our relationships, whether with others or ourselves, by nurturing and enriching them. As nature awakens, we're encouraged to explore self-love, emotional growth, and the beauty that surrounds us.

Materials:

- Matches or a lighter
- A pink candle
- Pen and paper
- A small glass jar with a lid
- A small piece of rose quartz
- Dried rose petals
- Dried lavender buds
- White or brown sugar

Directions:

Begin in a serene, quiet space and light the pink candle, allowing its gentle glow to envelop the room. Take a few deep breaths to anchor yourself in the present moment. Here, in the soft radiance of the full Pink Moon, set your intention clearly for self-love and inner peace.

Write positive affirmations or self-love mantras on the piece of paper, allowing your intentions to flow from your heart to the page. Fold it and place it in the jar. Layer the jar with the rose quartz crystal, dried rose petals, lavender buds, and a sprinkling of white or brown sugar. With each addition, envision self-love growing stronger within you, radiating outwards.

Seal the jar with wax from the pink candle, symbolizing the protective, loving light that surrounds and supports your self-love journey. Leave the jar under the full Pink Moon's gentle light to charge it with self-love energy overnight. Keep the jar in a visible spot in your home. Whenever you need a boost of self-love, hold it in your hands and repeat your affirmations, feeling the loving energy you've cultivated filling your heart.

FULL FLOWER MOON

Flower Petal Bath Ritual for Beauty

In May, the full Flower Moon illuminates the sky, embodying the lush and abundant energy of spring in full bloom. During this phase, we embrace fertility, expansion, and the celebration of life's beauty. This moon invites us to embrace creativity, set intentions for growth and prosperity, and nurture our connections with nature and loved ones as we bask in the vibrancy of the season.

This bath ritual can be modified to feature any flowers you desire, but don't skip out on the hibiscus if possible. Not only does hibiscus improve skin tone and texture, but it will turn your bath water a gorgeous shade of pink while you soak (but don't worry, it won't stain the tub).

Materials:

- Matches or a lighter
- A white or pink candle
- 1 cup (240 g) pink Himalayan salt
- A handful of dried hibiscus
- A handful of fresh or dried rose petals
- A handful of fresh or dried chamomile
- Jasmine essential oil

Directions:

Create a tranquil atmosphere in your bathroom with soft lighting and calming music. Draw a warm bath. Light the candle and place it safely in the bathroom. Take a moment to set your intention and to express gratitude for nature's beauty and abundance. Add the pink Himalayan salt, rose petals, hibiscus, chamomile, and a few drops of jasmine essential oil to the bath water. As you do, visualize their vibrant energy infusing the water with love and appreciation.

Step into the bath, immersing yourself in the fragrant and colorful water. Reflect on the beauty of the natural world around you. Express gratitude for the abundance of life and the simple joys it brings. As you soak, imagine any negativity or stress being released into the water, leaving you renewed and refreshed. When you're ready, exit the bath, letting the water carry away any remaining tension. Allow yourself to drip dry. Safely extinguish the candle when you're done, feeling a deep sense of gratitude.

FULL STRAWBERRY MOON

Honey Blessing Ceremony for Gratitude

The full Strawberry Moon arrives in June, signifying the strawberry harvest season. It carries the energy of joy, abundance, and sweet beginnings. This moon is ideal for setting intentions related to relationships, growth, and savoring the sweetness of life. It encourages us to celebrate our achievements and nurture connections, much like the ripe strawberries of summer.

In this ritual, you'll tap into the magical properties of honey in a blessing ceremony. In rituals, honey is often used to attract positive energy, promote abundance, and strengthen the intention of spells. Its natural stickiness makes it an excellent ingredient for binding spells or sealing intentions. Agave syrup can also be used as a vegan alternative, as its sweet and viscous nature shares similar energetic associations with that of honey.

Materials:

- Photos of loved ones or items that represent happiness
- A piece of rose quartz
- A piece of citrine
- Matches or a lighter
- A candle
- Fresh strawberries
- A small plate
- A jar of honey or agave syrup

Directions:

Find a quiet space and create a small altar with photos of loved ones or items that represent happiness, rose quartz for love, citrine for joy, and a lit candle. Sit in front of the altar, taking a moment to center yourself. Close your eyes and express gratitude for the sweetness of life and the blessings it brings. Reflect on the moments, people, and experiences that have filled your life with joy.

Cup a few strawberries in your hands and offer them to the universe as a symbol of your appreciation for life's gifts. Place them on a small plate on the altar. Open the jar of honey and drizzle a small amount over the strawberries while saying, "May the sweetness of life flow, and may I savor every moment." Slowly eat the strawberries one by one, relishing their taste and texture. Extinguish the candle, giving thanks for the blessings you've experienced thus far and for those that are still on the way. Keep the honey jar on your altar as a reminder to savor each moment.

FULL BUCK MOON

Tiger's Eye Talisman Ritual for Inner Strength

The full Buck Moon, rising in July, derives its name from the growing antlers of buck deer. It embodies an energy of strength, growth, and action. This moon is a potent time for setting intentions related to personal development, pursuing goals, and taking assertive steps toward your dreams. It encourages you to harness your inner power and make bold moves.

In this ritual, you'll learn how to turn a tiger's eye crystal into a talisman for inner strength, giving you the courage to face down challenges. Tiger's eye is known for its protective and grounding properties, and is often used for enhancing confidence, mental clarity, and bravery.

Materials:

- A piece of tiger's eye
- Pen and paper
- A small pouch or cloth to carry your talisman

Directions:

Find a peaceful, quiet space where you won't be disturbed. Close your eyes and take several deep breaths to ground yourself. Visualize a golden light surrounding you, filling you with warmth and courage. On the piece of paper, write down your intention for inner strength. Be specific about the areas of your life where you'd like to take action, whether it's in your career, relationships, or with your health.

Next, hold the tiger's eye crystal in your dominant hand. Picture your inner strength growing, filling you with a radiant, golden light that matches the energy of the crystal. Hold the crystal to your solar plexus chakra (upper abdomen) and say, "I am strong. I am capable. I am fearless."

Finally, carefully place the crystal and the intention paper in the pouch or cloth. This pouch will serve as a talisman of your newfound inner strength and resilience. Carry it with you wherever you go, and whenever you require a boost of power, simply hold the crystal in your hand, close your eyes, and reconnect with its energy to banish self-doubt.

FULL STURGEON MOON

Water Scrying Ritual for Intuitive Insights

The full Sturgeon Moon appears in August, named for the plentiful sturgeon fish found in the Great Lakes of North America during this time of year. Its energy is one of abundance, fruition, and reflection. This moon is an excellent time for gaining clarity in your emotions and intentions. It encourages you to navigate the currents of life with wisdom and abundance, just as sturgeons swim with purpose in the water.

In this ritual, you'll learn the art of scrying to honor your intuition. Scrying is a versatile divination method that involves gazing into a reflective surface, such as a mirror, crystal, or water, to receive spiritual messages.

Materials:

- A dark-colored bowl
- Filtered or purified water
- A piece of moonstone
- A pen and a journal or notebook

Directions:

Choose a serene and quiet outdoor location on a moonlit night, preferably near a natural water source if possible. Fill the dark-colored bowl with clean water. Place it on a stable surface. Hold the moonstone in your hand and take a moment to connect with its lunar energy. Feel its cool, soothing vibrations and set your intention, asking for intuitive insights from the full Sturgeon Moon.

Sit comfortably beside the bowl, allowing your body to relax and your mind to clear. Gaze into the water's surface, focusing your attention on the gentle ripples created by the Moon's reflection. Keep the moonstone in your other hand or place it near the bowl. Allow your gaze to become soft and unfocused. As you peer into the water, let your mind wander. Pay attention to any images, symbols, or thoughts that arise. Trust your intuition and let it flow. When you feel you've received insights or guidance, thank the Moon for its assistance. Record your experiences and insights in a journal or notebook, as these messages may offer valuable guidance in the days ahead.

FULL CORN MOON

Apple Harvest Ritual for Abundance

The full Corn Moon shines in September, named for the corn harvest. Its energy resonates with abundance, gratitude, and completion. This moon is a perfect time to set intentions for reaping the rewards of your hard work, expressing thanks, and embracing the fullness of life. It encourages reflection on the cycles of growth and the culmination of goals.

Note: The full moon closest to the fall equinox is called the Harvest Moon, which can occur in September or October. So, the Harvest Moon can be the full Corn Moon if it falls in September, but about every three years, it falls in October. When the October full moon is not a Harvest Moon, it is known as the Hunter's Moon.

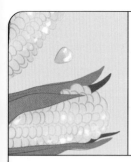

Materials:

- A ripe apple
- A small knife (optional)
- A plate

Directions:

On the evening of the full Corn Moon, prepare for this ritual in a quiet and serene area. Wash and dry the apple thoroughly. Sit in a calm, peaceful space near a window where moonlight can filter through. Using your fingernails or a sharp, small knife, gently etch symbols or words of gratitude and abundance into the apple's skin without breaking it. You can also trace the words or symbols on the apple with your finger if that feels more comfortable for you.

During this process, express your heartfelt thanks for the richness and prosperity you've experienced in your life. Place the carved apple on plate near the window sill, allowing the apple to absorb the Moon's energy throughout the night.

The following day, consume the apple, taking each bite mindfully and consciously appreciating it as a representation of the rewards you've earned through your hard work. Finally, take the apple core and return it to the earth, burying it in your garden or a potted plant. This act symbolizes your connection with the cycle of nature and the renewal of the earth.

FULL HUNTER MOON

Cord-Cutting Ritual for Release

The full Hunter Moon, gracing the skies in October, carries an energy of reflection, harvest, and preparation. Named for the time when hunters gather game for the coming winter, it's an ideal period to set intentions for self-reflection, gratitude, and readiness. This moon encourages us to assess our gains and prepare for the colder, quieter months ahead.

In this cord-cutting ritual, you'll be asked what needs to be released in your life in order for you to thrive. If you've been holding on to energetic baggage, now is the time to let go.

Materials:

- A piece of obsidian
- A black or dark-colored string or ribbon
- Matches or a lighter
- Pen and paper
- A fireproof dish or holder

Directions:

Find a serene outdoor spot under the moonlight or choose a quiet indoor area with dim lighting to create a contemplative atmosphere. Begin by holding the obsidian crystal in your hands, focusing on its detoxifying properties. This crystal's energy helps you engage in honest introspection.

Reflect on the things you need to release in your life, whether they are negative emotions, attachments, or habits that no longer serve you. Once these are clear in your mind, put your crystal aside and hold up the black or dark-colored string or ribbon in front of you. This represents the "cord" connecting you to these attachments.

Safely light one end of the cord and place it in the fireproof dish or holder as you affirm your intention for a fresh start, saying, "I release and let go. I am free." As it burns, visualize the negative attachments and energies you're releasing being transformed into smoke and rising to the Moon for cleansing. Once the cord has cooled, bury it in the earth, returning it to the ground as a symbol of your commitment to letting go.

FULL BEAVER MOON

Practical Tarot Spread for Preparedness

The full Beaver Moon appears in November, named for beavers preparing for winter. It embodies an energy of industriousness, planning, and building. This moon is an excellent time to set intentions related to organization, nesting, and fortifying your resources for the colder months ahead. It encourages careful preparation and creating a cozy, secure environment in various aspects of life.

In this tarot spread, you'll find insights into where to focus your attention to optimize your efforts, along with practical strategies to navigate obstacles. The cards drawn can provide guidance on organizing your life, whether it's in the physical realm or in mental and emotional spaces.

Materials:

- Your preferred tarot deck

Directions:

Begin by finding a quiet and comfortable space where you won't be disturbed. Hold your tarot deck and meditate on your intention to receive practical guidance as you make your winter preparations. Shuffle the cards, connecting with your purpose, and when the connection feels strong, cut the deck and draw three cards, placing them face down in a row.

Turn over the first card, which represents "The Current Situation." Reflect on the question: "What aspects of my life need attention as I prepare for the winter months?"

Turn over the second card, which signifies "Challenges to Address." Contemplate the question: "What obstacles or challenges may arise during the winter season, and how can I overcome them?"

Finally, reveal the third card, representing "Guidance and Focus." Meditate on the question: "What should I focus on and embrace to ensure a harmonious winter season?"

Take your time to interpret the cards' meanings and their guidance. Whenever you feel lost, lean into your intuition. Journal any insights and intentions for later reflection.

FULL COLD MOON

Cozy Tea Ritual for Introspection

In December, the full Cold Moon's arrival ushers in the winter's chill and an energy of inner reflection and rest. This moon offers a perfect opportunity to set intentions focused on self-nurturing, seeking solace, and illumination during the season's darkest days.

To honor this energy, create a personal ritual where you can envelop yourself in a cozy blanket and sip a warm cup of tea. This quiet moment of introspection will not only afford you some necessary alone time, but help you tune in to your innate wisdom.

Materials:

- Loose-leaf tea of your choice
- Teapot of infuser
- A pen and a journal
- Warm blanket or shawl

Directions:

Choose a loose-leaf tea for this ritual. Herbal teas such as chamomile, lavender, or peppermint are excellent options, but feel free to select your favorite. Boil water and prepare your tea in a teapot or infuser. As the tea steeps, take a few deep breaths to center yourself and set your intention for introspection during the full Cold Moon. Pour a cup of tea and wrap yourself in a warm blanket or shawl.

Hold the cup in your hands, feeling its warmth and comfort. Sip the tea slowly and mindfully, allowing its flavors and warmth to fill you. With each sip, turn your attention inward. Reflect on the past year, your goals, and what you wish to release or transform. Take your journal and pen and write down any insights, emotions, or thoughts that arise, letting your thoughts flow freely onto the pages. Continue sipping your tea and writing until you feel a sense of closure or clarity. Trust your intuition in knowing when it's time to conclude the ritual and give thanks to the universe for its guidance.

BLUE MOON

Butterfly Blue Pea Ritual for Embracing Change

A blue moon commonly refers to when we have an extra full moon in a calendar month or season. And contrary to what its name suggests, it's not really blue! Since blue moons only occur once every 2–3 years, they are believed to have a rare and unique energy, often associated with change and unexpected events. That said, blue moons offer a chance to break habits, set new intentions, and reflect on the unexpected twists and turns life may bring.

Materials:

- Butterfly blue pea flowers (fresh or dried)
- Clear glass or bowl
- Filtered or purified water
- Pen and paper
- Your favorite crystals (optional)
- Matches or a lighter
- A blue or white candle

Directions:

Find a peaceful outdoor spot where you can view the Moon, or create a serene atmosphere indoors. Place the butterfly blue pea flowers in a clear glass or bowl and pour water over them. As the flowers slowly turn the water blue, envision it as a reflection of the transformative energy of the blue moon. Sit comfortably and gaze at the Moon, focusing on its radiant glow. Write down what you wish to transform or release from your life during this blue moon. Place the paper into the blue-tinted water. Close your eyes for a few moments, visualizing the changes you desire.

When ready, light your candle as a beacon of transformation and allow it to burn throughout the ritual. Spend some time in quiet reflection, feeling the moon's energy infusing your intentions with its power. When you're ready to conclude, thank the Moon for its guidance and support. Pour the water onto the earth, symbolizing the release of what no longer serves you. Allow the candle to burn out on its own or safely extinguish it, knowing that the blue moon's transformative energy will continue to work in your life.

BLACK MOON

Charcoal Ritual for Manifestation

A black moon is a rare event when there are two new moons in a calendar month. During a new moon, the Moon is between the Earth and the Sun, so it appears almost invisible in the night sky. It's not actually black, but it's not visible to us. A black moon symbolizes new beginnings and hidden potential, intensifying the inward, contemplative energy that new moons typically bring. It's a great time for setting intentions, manifesting desires, and tapping into hidden strengths. In this ritual, you'll use activated charcoal powder to represent the darkness of this phase and your inner magic.

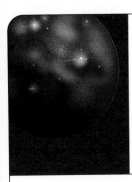

Materials:

- Matches or a lighter
- A black candle
- Pen and paper
- A fireproof dish or holder
- Activated charcoal powder or capsules

Directions:

To perform this ritual, create a sacred and dimly lit space where you can focus your energy. Light the black candle, focusing on its flame as a symbol of the potential for new beginnings and manifestations during the black moon. On the small piece of paper, write down your desires, goals, and intentions. Be specific and clear about what you wish to manifest in your life. Place the paper in the fireproof dish or holder.

Now, take the activated charcoal powder and use it to encircle your written intentions, visualizing the darkness enhancing their manifestation power as you do so. If you're using charcoal capsules, break them apart to release the powder.

Carefully light the paper with the black candle's flame, then return it to the fireproof dish or holder. Allow it to burn completely, sending your intentions into the universe. As the paper turns to ash, close your eyes and take a few deep breaths, feeling a sense of empowerment and alignment with your desires. When you're ready, extinguish the black candle, symbolizing the completion of the ritual.

CALM AND CENTERED

SOLAR ECLIPSE

Sound Healing Ritual for Inner Peace

In astrology, a solar eclipse is essentially a supercharged new moon, representing a significant turning point or bold new beginning. It occurs when the Moon passes between the Earth and the Sun, temporarily blocking out the Sun's light. Solar eclipses are said to bring about sudden and dramatic changes to our lives. They can set us off in a direction we may have never considered before, or open our eyes to opportunities we've previously ignored. Since eclipse energy can be unpredictable, it's best to avoid manifestation practices at this time. Instead, focus on nourishing self-care rituals that can soothe your mind, body, and soul.

Materials:

- A singing bowl, wind chimes, or a calming music playlist

Directions:

Select a sound instrument for the ritual such as Tibetan singing bowls, wind chimes, or a calming music playlist featuring nature sounds or crystal bowls. Close your eyes and take a few deep breaths to center yourself. Set the intention to release stress and find inner peace. Begin playing your chosen instruments or music. Focus your attention on the soothing sounds, allowing them to wash over you.

Starting from your toes, mentally scan your body for any tension. With each sound, imagine the vibrations melting away stress and filling you with tranquility. As you immerse in the sound, visualize a serene, peaceful scene—a calm lake, a lush forest, or a refreshing meadow. Whisper or think positive affirmations related to inner peace, such as,

"I AM CALM AND CENTERED,"

or,

"MY MIND IS AT EASE."

Sync your breath with the sounds. Inhale deeply as the sounds rise and exhale slowly as they fall. After a few minutes, gradually bring your awareness back to the present moment. Open your eyes, feeling refreshed and ready to flow with change.

LUNAR ECLIPSE

Yoga Flow Ritual for Grounding

A lunar eclipse is a special kind of full moon that occurs when the Earth comes between the Sun and the Moon, casting a shadow on the Moon. It represents a powerful moment of transformation and change, often revealing hidden truths or resulting in an important ending or breakthrough. The epiphanies or "a-ha" moments we experience during this lunation can be sudden and intense, adding a sense of upheaval to our lives. That said, a grounding exercise can be useful in providing stability amid major change.

Note: It's recommended to skip manifestation practices during an eclipse because they can bring unpredictable energies that may result in unexpected outcomes.

Materials:

- A yoga mat
- Comfortable, flexible clothing

Directions:

Set up your yoga mat in a clear, peaceful space. Stand up and close your eyes. Take a few deep breaths to quiet your mind and connect with your physical body. Begin your yoga flow by moving into Mountain Pose (Tadasana). Start in a standing position with your feet hip-width apart. Ground your feet firmly into the earth, lengthen your spine, and relax your shoulders. Take deep breaths, feeling the energy of the earth supporting you. Hold this pose for 3–5 breaths.

Next, move into Tree Pose (Vrksasana). Shift your weight to your right foot. Lift your left foot and place the sole against your inner right thigh, toes pointing down. Bring your hands to your heart in a prayer position. Find your balance and visualize your roots extending into the ground. Hold for 3–5 breaths and switch sides.

Lastly, come into Child's Pose (Balasana). Kneel on the floor, sit back on your heels, and extend your arms forward, forehead resting on the mat. Sink into this resting pose, surrendering any tension or worries to the earth. Breathe deeply and hold for as long as you like. Repeat the sequence if desired. Throughout this ritual, focus on your breath and the sensation of being anchored to the earth. It's a powerful way to stay connected and grounded during a lunar eclipse.

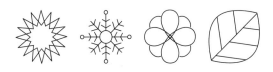

SEASONAL RITUALS

While lunar and zodiac rituals help us tap into the cosmic energies on a month-to-month basis, seasonal rituals offer us a different kind of perspective—one that's more about the big picture. Every few months, as the seasons change, we're presented with this opportunity to pause, reflect, and recalibrate our intentions. We're checking in with ourselves—asking questions like: What energies are we trying to call in? What do we need to release? How can we realign our lives with our deepest truths and desires?

And here's the really cool part: by aligning ourselves with these seasonal rhythms, we're not just tapping into some random cosmic energy—we're tapping into the very heartbeat of the Earth itself. We're syncing up with the natural cycles of life, death, and rebirth that have been happening since the dawn of time.

So whether it's spring, summer, fall, or winter, think of seasonal rituals as quarterly cosmic tune-ups for the soul. They help us stay grounded, centered, and connected to something greater than ourselves. And hey, in a world that can sometimes feel chaotic and overwhelming, isn't that exactly what we need?

SPRING

Garden Blessing Ritual for Honoring the Earth

Spring, a season of renewal and rebirth, ushers in new life and growth after the dormancy of winter. As the earth awakens, fresh greenery and vibrant flowers emerge, symbolizing rejuvenation, fertility, and transformation. This season is perfect for embarking on a new beginning and is marked by fresh ideas, innovative approaches, and a readiness to let go of the old to nurture new growth in our lives. Reflect on the intentions you'd like to sow during this season and use this garden blessing ritual to help them bloom.

Materials:

- A garden space or a potted plant
- Matches or a lighter
- A green or white candle
- A bowl of water with rose petals

Directions:

Select a serene natural spot, whether in a garden or by a balcony or window sill with potted plants, where you can deeply connect with nature. Stand barefoot on the earth, feeling its grounding energy beneath you. Take a few deep breaths to center yourself and light a green or white candle, representing life and purity. Place it beside your chosen space.

Dip your fingers into the bowl of water with rose petals. As you walk around your garden or gently touch your potted plant, sprinkle the water as an offering to nourish the earth. Pause at each plant, expressing gratitude for its presence and the abundance it will provide this season. Shower your plants with words of encouragement and blessings, fostering their growth and vitality. Visualize your garden thriving with vibrant energy and lush foliage. To conclude the ritual, safely extinguish the candle and offer thanks to the earth for its endless gifts.

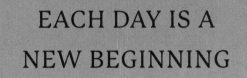

EACH DAY IS A
NEW BEGINNING

SUMMER

Sunrise Meditation for Renewed Vitality

Summer, with its radiant warmth and extended daylight, embodies a season of vitality and abundance. It marks the peak of the yearly cycle, a time of growth and fruition. Summer's energy encourages us to revel in the pleasures of life, bask in the Sun's nourishing glow, and savor moments of joy and connection. In this ritual, you'll learn how to harness the revitalizing power of the Sun to supercharge your spirit and honor the light within.

Materials:

- Comfortable clothing
- A piece of sunstone

Directions:

Find a serene outdoor spot with a clear view of the eastern horizon where you can witness the sunrise. Wake up early and dress comfortably. Hold the sunstone crystal in your hand, feeling its warm energy. Come to a seated position facing the east, close your eyes, and take a few deep breaths. As the first rays of the Sun peek over the horizon, visualize its warm and vibrant energy washing over you, infusing you with renewed vitality.

With your eyes still closed, silently repeat affirmations such as,

"I AM FILLED WITH ENERGY AND VITALITY,"

or,

"EACH DAY IS A NEW BEGINNING, FULL OF POTENTIAL."

As the Sun rises higher in the sky, imagine a golden light within you growing stronger and larger with each breath until you are completely filled with light. When ready, open your eyes and notice how recharged and alive you feel. Carry this sense of renewed energy and optimism with you throughout the day, keeping the sunstone close as a reminder of your connection to the Sun's revitalizing power.

FALL

Foliage Divination
Ritual for Clarity

Fall, a season of transition, bears the energy of change and reflection. It plays a vital role in the cyclical rhythm of nature, marking the shift from growth to rest. As leaves change and fall, it prompts us to let go what no longer serves us, inviting introspection and preparation for the coming winter. During this time, we are encouraged to express gratitude for the harvest, find beauty in impermanence, and embrace change as a natural part of life. In this ritual, fall foliage becomes a powerful divination tool, guiding you to the answers you seek.

Materials:

- Colorful fall leaves
- A pen

Directions:

Take a mindful walk in a park or woods, gathering fallen leaves that resonate with you. Find a secluded outdoor spot to perform the ritual and take a moment to ground yourself with deep breaths (note: during windy weather, it's best to perform this ritual indoors). Bring to mind any questions or intentions you seek guidance on, then write them down on the leaves, one by one. Gather the leaves in your hands and say, "With each leaf that flies, answers will rise," then scatter them gently.

Observe which leaves land closest to you or group together, using your intuition to interpret their positions and meanings. As you conclude the ritual, express gratitude to the natural world for its guidance. Leave the leaves where they are as an offering or take those that are significant to you to display on an altar. Take some time to reflect on the insights gained during this practice and consider how to apply this newfound wisdom to your life.

Winter, a season of stillness and solitude, carries an energy of introspection and rest. Its significance lies in providing the earth with a much-needed pause for renewal and regeneration. Winter's energy invites us to turn inward, nurturing our inner worlds, and finding beauty in simplicity. It's a time for reflection, hibernation, and fostering clarity in our intentions for the upcoming year. In this ritual, you'll create an altar to honor Skadi—the Norse goddess of winter—to imbue you with endurance and resilience this season.

Materials:

- Smoke cleansing tools (optional)
- A small table or surface
- A white or silver altar cloth
- Winter-themed decorations such as pinecones, snowflakes, or evergreen sprigs
- Clear quartz or snowfall obsidian crystals
- A small bowl or chalice filled with ice cubes
- A white or silver candle to represent the goddess's presence
- Matches or a lighter
- A small image or statue of Skadi, if available

Directions:

Create a flat, stable, tranquil space for your altar. Cleanse your space through a smoke cleansing ceremony or a visualization technique. Drape your table with a white or silver altar cloth, signifying winter. Arrange the winter-themed decorations, clear quartz or snowflake obsidian crystals, and bowl of ice on the altar. Position the candle at the center and light it, symbolizing the goddess's presence and warmth amid winter's cold. If you have an image or statue of Skadi, place it on the altar to honor her.

Offer a prayer or affirmation to Skadi, such as, "Skadi, winter's queen, grant me the strength to endure the cold. With your guidance, I navigate this season with resilience and grace." Spend a few moments at your altar, soaking in the goddess's presence. When you're ready, extinguish the candle. Return to the altar whenever you need a moment of solitude.

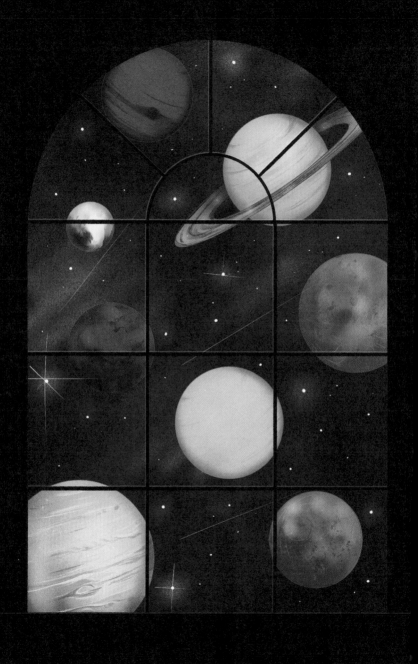

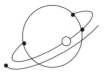

PLANETARY RITUALS

When aligning with the cosmos for self-care, we often focus on the Sun and the Moon as our guiding lights, but let's not forget about the wisdom of the other planets. Each planet has its own unique qualities and influences. Venus, for instance, is all about love and beauty, while Mars is the fiery planet of passion and action. By tapping into these planetary energies, you can focus on specific areas of personal growth and well-being.

In this section, you'll find a variety of rituals designed to invoke and honor the energy of each planet. As mentioned in the planetary calendar on page 14, you can time these rituals to coincide with planetary movements through the zodiac signs, retrograde periods, or specific days of the week. Choose what resonates with you and be consistent. Regularity in your practices can enhance your connection with planetary energies, creating a stronger bond over time.

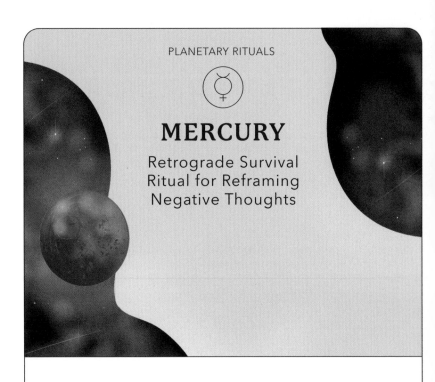

MERCURY

Retrograde Survival
Ritual for Reframing
Negative Thoughts

In astrology, Mercury is the celestial messenger of the zodiac, ruling over communication, intellect, and information processing. When this planet goes retrograde, its energy takes a bit of a twist. During these periods, Mercury appears to move backward in the sky from our Earthly perspective. This cosmic illusion symbolizes a time when Mercury's energy turns inward, and its usual smooth-flowing qualities may become disrupted, leading to challenges in communication, travel, and technology.

However, there's a silver lining. Mercury retrograde offers a period for introspection and reflection, allowing you to revisit past issues and make necessary adjustments. Use this period to tie up loose ends, clarify misunderstandings, and strengthen your adaptability.

Materials:

- A lavender scented candle or lavender oil diffuser (optional)
- Pen and paper
- A piece of blue sodalite

Directions:

Find a quiet, comfortable space and light a lavender-scented candle or diffuse lavender oil to create a calming atmosphere. You can also dab a few drops of a diluted essential oil mixture on your pulse points, such as your temples, wrists, and neck (a common dilution ratio is 2–3 drops of essential oil per teaspoon of carrier oil such as jojoba oil). Close your eyes, taking slow and deliberate breaths to center yourself.

Identify a negative thought you've been having recently related to communication and write it down on the piece of paper, such as, "I never know the right words to say." Hold the blue sodalite crystal in your hands and meditate with it, allowing its soothing energy to help you release your limiting beliefs.

Now, revisit your initial statement and rewrite it in a positive and empowering manner, such as, "It is easy for me to articulate my thoughts and feelings." With your eyes closed, visualize this positive statement becoming your new reality, reinforced by the truth-enhancing attributes of the blue sodalite. Keep the crystal where you'll encounter it daily as a reminder of your newfound mindset and your ability to communicate confidently and effectively.

CONFIDENT
AND CAPABLE

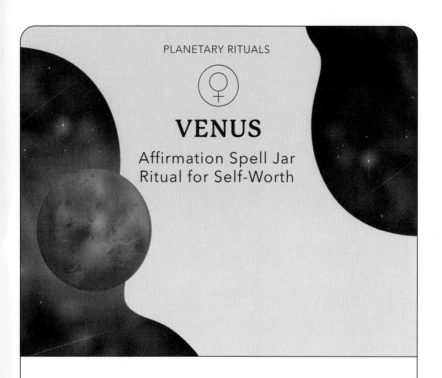

VENUS

Affirmation Spell Jar Ritual for Self-Worth

Venus is the planet of love and beauty. Its energy encourages us to appreciate aesthetics, seek pleasure, and form connections with others. As it moves through the zodiac signs, our values and preferences in love and relationships can shift, reflecting the different qualities of each sign. For instance, we may crave passionate connections when Venus is in Aries versus a more practical approach to romance when Venus is in Virgo.

Additionally, Venus retrograde is an excellent time for introspection regarding matters of the heart, self-worth, and values. Use this transit to review past relationships, assess your desires, and reevaluate what brings you joy. This spell jar ritual for self-worth is a wonderful way to honor Venus, fostering self-love and confidence through daily affirmations.

Materials:

- · Matches or a lighter (optional)
- · Pink candles or rose quartz crystals
- · Pink or green paper
- · A pen
- · Pink or green ribbon
- · A small glass jar with a lid

Directions:

Choose a peaceful space to perform the ritual. Light the pink candles or place rose quartz crystals nearby to amplify the energies of love and self-worth. On the pink or green paper, write down positive affirmations about yourself. These could include statements such as,

"I AM WORTHY OF LOVE,"

"I AM CONFIDENT AND CAPABLE,"

or,

"I RADIATE BEAUTY INSIDE AND OUT."

Roll up each affirmation individually and tie them with a piece of pink or green ribbon. Place these affirmation scrolls in the jar one by one, infusing each with your intent for greater self-worth.

Close the jar's lid gently but securely. Hold the jar in your hands and visualize a warm, pink or green light enveloping it. Imagine this light representing the self-love you wish to cultivate. Each day, open the jar and select one affirmation scroll at random. Carry it with you or place it somewhere visible. Throughout the day, focus on this affirmation, repeating it to yourself as a reminder of your self-worth and inner beauty. Continue this daily ritual for as long as you feel necessary to boost your self-esteem and honor the energies of Venus.

MARS

Candle Ritual for Overcoming Obstacles

Mars rules over our drive, ambition, and assertiveness. Its transits can bring forth bursts of energy, motivation, and even occasional impatience or aggression. Connecting with Mars' energy empowers us to face obstacles head-on and take bold action, making it an essential force for achieving success and personal growth. Since Mars is associated with the element of fire and the color red, using a red candle in a flame gazing ritual is an excellent way to honor its energy and work through obstacles.

Materials:

- A pin or small tool for carving (optional)
- A red candle
- Matches or a lighter

Directions:

Find a serene and uncluttered space to perform the ritual. Using a pin or your fingernails, carve the symbol of Mars (a circle with an arrow pointing right on the diagonal) onto the red candle. As you carve this symbol, focus your intention on overcoming obstacles and igniting your inner strength.

Light the red candle and begin your meditation by gazing into the flame, drawing the fiery essence of Mars into your being. Close your eyes and, in the candle's glow, visualize yourself filled with courage, determination, and vitality. See yourself confidently surmounting challenges.

Accept the courage and strength Mars offers, knowing that you are the master of your path, able to conquer any obstacles that come your way. When you feel fully charged with bravery and determination, open your eyes and extinguish the candle safely. Leave the ritual space, carrying this invigorated energy with you into the world. Use it to face your challenges, create your path, and embrace your victories.

♃

JUPITER

Ritual Bath for Luck & Expansion

Jupiter, in the realm of astrology, governs expansion, growth, and good fortune. It influences various aspects of our lives, from our beliefs and philosophy to opportunities for abundance and prosperity. Connecting with the energy of Jupiter through a ritual bath for luck and expansion is a wonderful way to honor its presence. This ritual can help you align your intentions with Jupiter's expansive and fortunate energies, supporting personal growth and a greater receptivity to opportunities. It's a practice that invites you to embrace a positive, optimistic outlook on life while fostering an open mindset.

Materials:

- Matches or a lighter
- A yellow or purple candle
- 1 cup (240 g) Epsom salts
- 0.8 oz (25 g) dried garden sage leaves
- Jasmine essential oil
- A small piece of amethyst

Directions:

Create a peaceful atmosphere in your bathroom by dimming the lights. Light the candle and set it in a safe place, then draw a bath. As the water flows, visualize it as a river of opportunity and abundance, welcoming the blessings of Jupiter. Add the Epsom salts, dried garden sage leaves, and a couple drops of jasmine essential oil to the water.

Stir the bath water clockwise with your hand, focusing on your intentions for luck and expansion. Hold the small piece of amethyst in your hands and close your eyes. Imagine yourself stepping into a world of possibilities, then carefully step into the tub. Let go of any fears or doubts as you immerse yourself in the water. Picture yourself expanding and thriving and feel the energy of Jupiter's blessings surrounding you. Trust that luck is on your side.

As you finish the bath, visualize any obstacles or negativity being washed away and dissolving into the water. Step out of the bath and allow yourself to air dry. Safely extinguish the candle and give thanks to Jupiter for its guidance.

SATURN

Freezer Ritual
to Thwart
Procrastination

In astrology, Saturn governs responsibility, discipline, and structure. This planet pushes us to work hard and has gained a reputation for being the "taskmaster" of the zodiac. As it moves through different zodiac signs, its energy subtly shifts to influence our lives. For example, in practical Capricorn, Saturn's home sign, it emphasizes ambition and hard work. When it transitions into innovative Aquarius, it encourages us to apply structure to our unconventional ideas. To harness Saturn's energy, consider a freezer spell to stop procrastination dead in its tracks.

Materials:

- A few small pieces of paper
- A pen
- An ice cube tray or a couple of small paper cups

Directions:

Find a quiet space where you won't be disturbed. Begin by writing down specific ways in which you tend to procrastinate on small pieces of paper, such as, "Scrolling on social media," or, "Avoiding important tasks." If you have an ice cube tray, place each paper in individual compartments. Alternatively, you can use small paper cups. Pour the water over the papers while focusing on your intention to eliminate procrastination. Visualize yourself becoming more productive and efficient.

Carefully place the ice cube tray or cups in the freezer. As you close the freezer door, say a few words to affirm your intention to work through procrastination such as, "I am excited to get things done and see the results." As the water freezes, it will symbolize freezing procrastination's hold over you. Each piece of paper is now encased in ice, preventing these habits from influencing your actions. Leave the ice in the freezer until you notice a significant shift in your procrastination tendencies. When you feel more productive and in control of your time, you can choose to thaw and dispose of the ice, or break the ice cubes to sever the energetic connection to these negative behaviors for good.

URANUS

Meditation for Sudden Inspiration

In astrology, Uranus embodies innovation, liberation, and rebellion. Its presence signifies sudden changes, unconventional thinking, and groundbreaking ideas. As Uranus transits through zodiac signs, it ushers in unique energies. For example, in Taurus, it prompts shifts in financial perspectives and eco-consciousness. Embracing Uranian energy entails adapting to change with courage and open-mindedness. The benefit lies in breaking free from stagnant routines and finding inspiration in unexpected places.

To harness this energy, meditation is a powerful tool. By carving out time for meditation, we cultivate stillness in a rapidly changing world, allowing sudden insights to surface. Whether through focused visualizations or deep breathing exercises, meditation enhances our receptivity to Uranus' transformative influence, fostering innovation and adaptability in our lives.

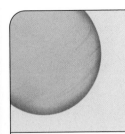

Materials:

- A pen and a journal
- A small piece of labradorite

Directions:

Find a quiet and comfortable space. Sit or lie down with your back straight and close your eyes. Keep your labradorite crystal nearby. Begin with deep, calming breaths. Inhale slowly through your nose, allowing your lungs to fill completely, and exhale through your mouth, releasing tension. Picture a vibrant electric-blue light surrounding your body. Envision it growing brighter with each breath.

Hold the labradorite in your hand. Feel its cool energy and imagine it amplifying your connection to Uranus' innovative influence. Visualize your third eye (between your eyebrows) as a channel for Uranian energy, opening to receive insights. Mentally or verbally ask Uranus for guidance and inspiration. Continue to breathe deeply, remaining open to whatever comes to mind. Keep a journal nearby to record any sudden inspiration. Write down your thoughts, even if they seem unconventional. Carry the newfound inspiration with you into your day, along with your piece of labradorite to continue sparking creative insights.

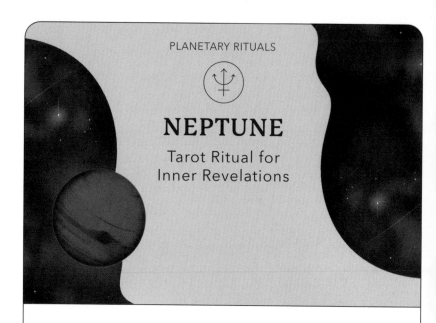

NEPTUNE

Tarot Ritual for Inner Revelations

Neptune is the planet of dreams, illusions, and intuition. Its energy is subtle, ethereal, and often associated with the unseen realms. Neptune governs our creativity, spirituality, and the mysteries of the subconscious mind. As it transits through the zodiac signs, it casts a dreamy and idealistic influence on our lives. When in the right alignment, Neptune can inspire artistic expression, heightened intuition, and a deep connection to the spiritual aspects of existence. However, its energy can also be elusive, leading to confusion, escapism, and delusions.

Harnessing Neptune's energy involves nurturing your intuition, embracing your artistic side, and seeking spiritual growth. It's about finding the balance between the dreamy and the practical aspects of life. This ritual is designed to tap into your intuitive wisdom with the guidance of Neptune. You'll draw three tarot cards to gain insights and messages from your inner self and the cosmos.

Materials:

- Matches or a lighter
- Candle or incense and a holder
- Your preferred tarot deck
- A pen and a journal

Directions:

Find a quiet, peaceful space where you won't be disturbed. Light a candle or incense of your choosing to set a serene atmosphere. Shuffle your tarot deck, focusing on your intention to receive intuitive guidance.

Draw the first card and place it on the left. This card represents your past experiences or influences related to your question. Reflect on its meaning and any past insights that connect to your current situation.

Draw the second card and place it in the center. This card signifies your current circumstances and the intuitive insights available to you at this moment. Meditate on its symbolism and how it relates to your question.

Draw the third card and place it on the right. This card offers insights into future possibilities and the path ahead. Consider how this card's message can guide you in making decisions.

Analyze each card's imagery, symbolism, and your own intuitive feelings. Trust your inner wisdom and Neptune's influence to reveal profound insights. Record your thoughts in a journal, allowing these intuitive messages to guide your path.

PLANETARY RITUALS

PLUTO

Letter Ritual for Compassionate Release

Pluto plays a transformative role in astrology, representing rebirth, regeneration, and profound change. Its energy influences us by delving into the depths of our subconscious, revealing hidden truths, and catalyzing personal evolution. As Pluto transits through the zodiac signs, it brings about intense, often cathartic experiences, dismantling old structures and paving the way for new beginnings. It pushes us to confront our fears and attachments, ultimately allowing us to shed old layers and emerge stronger and more authentic.

Working with Pluto's energy can be both challenging and empowering, offering a chance for profound self-discovery and rebirth. In this compassionate letter ritual, we'll explore and address your shadow self, that part of your psyche where hidden fears, desires, and past wounds reside.

Materials:

- Pen and paper

Directions:

Find a peaceful space to perform the ritual and gather your materials. Take a few deep breaths and ground yourself in the present moment. Start the letter by addressing your shadow self. Mention that you're writing to acknowledge the aspects of yourself you've kept hidden, those that have held you back or caused pain. Within the letter, respond to these questions:

- What aspects of my shadow self have I ignored or rejected?
- What behaviors, habits, or beliefs would I like to release?
- How can I acknowledge and forgive myself for past mistakes?
- What actions am I willing to take to grow and heal?

As you write, be compassionate and forgiving toward yourself, recognizing that you are a work in progress. After writing, take a moment to reflect on your letter's content. Express gratitude for the opportunity for growth. Fold the letter, and seal it in an envelope. You can choose to keep it or, when you're ready, safely burn or bury it as a symbol of your commitment to personal transformation.

AFFIRMATIONS

Affirmations are powerful statements that work to reprogram our thought patterns, guiding us toward a more positive and empowered mindset. By regularly repeating affirmations, we reinforce constructive beliefs about ourselves and our abilities. When it comes to self-care, these affirmations can serve as transformative tools, helping to nurture self-compassion, mindfulness, and personal growth.

The following affirmations are meticulously crafted to deepen your connection with the cosmos, acknowledge the changing seasons in life, and embrace your inner magic. They can be incorporated into spells, rituals, meditations, or any other energetic practice you desire. Use them to infuse your intentions with power and strength, and direct your focus toward your goals. I also recommend modifying the affirmations to your liking or crafting your own if you feel called to do so.

The constellations above remind me that even in darkness, there is a path to follow.

I honor the sacred cycles of life, knowing that when one door closes, another one opens, revealing new opportunities and growth.

I am a co-creator of my destiny, and my intentions manifest powerfully.

I release the need to control every outcome, allowing the universe to work its magic.

My relationships, friendships, career goals, and hobbies may look different than they were a few years ago and that's OK. I'm allowed to change.

Everything is unfolding in perfect timing.
I trust. I believe. I receive.

I release the fear of failure because
mistakes help me evolve. Learning to
navigate challenges only makes
me stronger, wiser, and more resilient.

I embrace the ever-changing seasons of my
life, finding beauty in each phase.

My heart and mind are open to
the magic of new beginnings.

I am so proud of my journey and how far
I've come. Acknowledging my daily progress
is just as important as celebrating
my big wins.

I am a magnet of blessings, and I am open to receiving the boundless gifts that life has in store for me.

I find peace in slowing down, allowing the world's simple wonders to fill my heart and enrich my soul.

*Happiness is a choice I choose.
I believe in my worthiness and know that the abundance, joy, and love I deserve is on its way to me.*

Just as the universe endlessly expands, so does my capacity to love and accept myself unconditionally.

*Even when life seems uncertain,
I trust that the universe has a plan for me and that what is meant for me will manifest at the right time.*

*I let go of the pressure to follow a set path
or conform to others' expectations.
I am the author of my own story and
choose to live my life authentically
and courageously.*

*I trust my intuition as a guiding light,
leading me toward choices that resonate
with my true self.*

*In this moment, I have everything
I need. My breath is my anchor.*

*I flow through life's transitions like a river,
guided by the wisdom of nature's
ebb and flow.*

*I have amazing things to offer the world,
and I'm ready to share my gifts in a way
that feels aligned with my soul.*

CONCLUSION

Dear reader,

In a universe this big, it's easy to feel small—like mere specks in the boundless expanse of space. Yet, for me, this realization has always held a touch of magic. Being a part of this vast world doesn't frighten me, it inspires me, and I hope this book has helped you lean into that same feeling. Just as the planets and stars follow their paths with purpose, we too must find our way through our life's journey with intention and awareness.

It's not always easy to navigate the various phases, from the highs of joy to the lows of hardship, but each stage tells a unique story and imparts valuable lessons. It's like turning the pages of a book—when one chapter ends, it's often bittersweet, yet necessary to start a new one. Though it may be hard to accept the end of a phase, it's in those moments of closure that we find the motivation and strength to begin anew.

As you move forward with your self-care practice, remember to embrace change as an integral part of your transformation. Just like the seasons shift, your self-care practice should continuously evolve to reflect your changing needs. So, keep your heart open to the twists and turns that life presents, as they are the catalysts for your personal growth. Know that you belong here and that the universe has got your back.

With love,

Katie

RECOMMENDED READING

Self-Love Crystals: Crystal Spells and Rituals for Magical Self-Care by Katie Huang (2024, Leaping Hare Press)

Transform your relationship with self-love by delving into the magical world of crystals. Filled with countless recipes and rituals for harnessing self-compassion and self-confidence, this book is a must-have for those looking to leave self-doubt behind.

Crystal Moods by Katie Huang (2023, The Book Shop Ltd)

Explore the connection between crystals and emotions with this interactive kit that includes seven foundational stones, a 120-page book, and full color chakra poster.

Luminous Dreams: Explore the Abundant Magic and Hidden Meanings in Your Dreams by Katie Huang (2022, Chronicle)

This beautifully illustrated, soothing guide invites readers to explore the world of dreams through a collection of bedtime rituals, dream symbols, and intuitive practices.

Crystal Zodiac: An Astrological Guide to Enhancing Your Life with Crystals by Katie Huang (2020, Houghton Mifflin)

For anyone new to the benefits of crystal healing and astrology, or for those who have been practicing for years, this book breaks down their practical, easy-to-use applications, showing how they powerfully work together to prioritize personal growth and mindfulness in the day-to-day.

INDEX

R

ABOUT THE AUTHOR & ILLUSTRATOR

Katie Huang is the founder of Love By Luna, a leading astrological lifestyle brand. With her extensive knowledge of astrology and crystal healing, she has written: *Self-Love Crystals: Crystal Spells and Rituals for Magical Self-Care, Crystal Moods, Crystal Zodiac: An Astrological Guide to Enhancing Your Life with Crystals,* and, *Luminous Dreams: Explore the Abundant Magic and Hidden Meanings in Your Dreams.*

Her insightful work has been featured in numerous publications such as Forbes, Cosmopolitan, Teen Vogue, and Marie Claire. As a wellness entrepreneur and mental health advocate, Katie is passionate about developing accessible tools for mindful living, and strives to empower individuals in their personal and spiritual growth. She resides in Santa Monica, California.

You can find her work at lovebyluna.co

Instagram: @lovebyluna

Phe Johnson is an illustrator based in Devon, UK. Her work takes inspiration from 90s/early 00s illustration and graphic design styles that she grew up with, as well as being inspired by slow living and mindful thinking.

Her work consists of product design for her online store, for which she creates products from printed goods to clothing, and freelance work with clients on various projects including album artwork, branding, logos, and custom illustrations for print.

You can find her work at phejohnson.com

Instagram: @phejohnson

Quarto

First published in 2024 by Leaping Hare Press
an imprint of The Quarto Group.
One Triptych Place, London, SE1 9SH
United Kingdom
T (0)20 7700 6700
www.Quarto.com

A catalogue record for this book is available
from the British Library.

ISBN 978-0-7112-9433-2
Ebook ISBN 978-0-7112-9434-9

10 9 8 7 6 5 4 3 2 1

Design by Hanri van Wyk

Printed in China

The information in this book is for
informational purposes only and should
not be treated as a substitute for
professional counselling, medical advice
or any medication or other treatment
prescribed by a medical practitioner;
always consult a medical professional.
Any use of the information in this book is
at the reader's discretion and risk.
The author and publisher make no
representations or warranties with
respect to the accuracy, completeness
or fitness for a particular purpose of the
contents of this book and exclude all
liability to the extent permitted by law for
any errors and omissions and for any
injury, loss, damage or expense suffered
by anyone arising out of the use, or
misuse, of the information in this book,
or any failure to take professional
medical advice.